Praise for The C

"The CREEI Process is enlightening, gr........ and formed by thousands of hours of time-tested research, and is a blessing to all of us who want to take a deeper dive into understanding the mysteries of our dreams and dreaming mind and still stay somewhat secretive about it. The CREEI Process is a blessing to all of us."
—Kelly Sullivan Walden, best-selling dream author

"An ingeniously simple dream questionnaire. [In the] CREEI Process the insight and practical usefulness which often bursts forth is surprisingly profound and mysteriously synchronous in its expression. [These] innovative techniques for bridging the inner world of intuition and creativity with the outer world of hard-nosed business acumen deserve the attention of both dream researchers and executives."
—Joseph Dillard, PhD, Psychotherapist

"[The CREEI Process is] a rapid, effective, and clinically useful body of information."
—Rima E. Laibow, MD, Psychiatrist

"The positive direction that I took and the continuing upward direction of my life can be directly attributed to using your clever CREEI Process."
—Lou Avitable, Production Manager at Brunswick Defense Corporation

The CREEI Process... makes sense and is easy for all of my clients to use.
—Nancy J. Swenson, State Penitentiary Psychologist

"A skeptic no more, I believe The CREEI Process has helped me tap into one of the greatest hidden sources of creative and self-realization available to us. The CREEI Process, when used properly, is the key to opening this door."
—Raul G., Former Los Angeles gang member

"The CREEI Process has been an effective resource both personally and professionally. It is worth the effort to learn and utilize the process."
—W. Clark Rex, PhD, Consulting Behavioral Scientist and CEO

"The CREEI Process is more objective and even quantifiable. [It] is particularly useful in pastoral or confidential situations. I know of few psychologists who have the 40 years of experience remembering and analyzing their own dreams as Dr. Kovalenko has done. He is truly an expert in this field."
—Kendall O. Price, PhD, Social Psychologist

"I have found The CREEI Process to be useful in coaching executive clients about work and life issues, in helping individuals think about their dreams, [and as] a useful tool in teaching students how to manage their own lives and attitudes. The process also has been helpful to me personally."
—Rex C. Mitchell, PhD, Professor of Management, California State University, Northridge

"Many of us who were in Vietnam have been through various sorts of treatments for lingering issues during that period. Most of them have not produced any significant results. I've found [The CREEI Process] to be very gratifying, helpful, insight-giving, and perception-building. It's been a big help."
—James Nesmith, Jr., Viet Nam War veteran and, at the time of his response, Vice-Commander of Post 8874 of the Veterans of Foreign Wars

PORTAL
to
MEANING

A Process for
Unlocking Dreams

Eugene N. Kovalenko
and Robert J. Thomsen

PAGE PUBLISHING, INC.
Conneaut Lake, PA

First Edition

PAGE PUBLISHING, INC. Conneaut Lake, PA

Printed in the United States of America

ISBN 978-1-64544-797-9 (pbk)
ISBN 978-1-64544-798-6 (digital)

Cover image: "The Light Within" by Eugene N. Kovalenko
and Emily Bartlett

Background image: "GREAT CHAIN" by Eugene N. Kovalenko

Editing and design by Michael Kovalenko

Dedications

Eugene Kovalenko:
A legacy to my family, beginning with my youngest
son, Johnny, to whom I made a promise.

Robert Thomsen:
To my wonderful wife, Michelle F. Thomsen.
You have been consistently supportive of the work
done to bring this CREEI Process to light.

Acknowledgments

In the effort to deal with significant dreams and better understand the language of the unconscious mind, we diverged from our professional backgrounds to seek deeper truths about the self and, hopefully, develop a method for inner transformation. Discussions about dreams often include sensive and personal feelings or experiences. Over the years, many new and wonderful individuals became part of our odyssey.

We are grateful for the contributions of many people to the development of THE CREEI PROCESS and the creation of this book, including the multitude of participants in workshops and seminars through the years. Each has contributed to this work in their own way and taught us about this remarkable process. Some examples are highlighted in the book, and we hope that by detailing their stories we have given sufficient credit, especially in APPENDIX E. A complete list of people who have contributed to the development of this process would be lengthy and no doubt leave out important names. Where we have neglected to acknowledge we ask forgiveness.

In the crucial early stages of CREEI development Lawrene Kovalenko, Howard E. Salisbury, Reed C. Durham, Sr., Robert Rees, John R. Howard, and a small group of wise and experienced members of Bel Air Presbyterian Church in Los Angeles all were helpful in many and various ways. Close friends and associates, Kendall Price, Clark Rex, and Rex Mitchell provided continuous feedback and support. Joseph Dillard has given enthusiastic and constant encouragement, knowledge, humor, experience and wisdom for many years. Arnold Mindell has consistently been an insightful respondent with any and all of our dreams.

We specifically thank Kelly Sullivan Walden for her support and touching example of what this process can do for even an experienced dream worker. Jim Wood provided financial and logistical support when it was greatly needed. Thank you to Joseph Dillard, Michelle Thomsen, Birgitta Kovalenko, Katya Kovalenko Smith, and Davis

Thomsen for invaluable comments on the form and substance of the manuscript.

We especially thank Michael Kovalenko for his persistence, patience, rigorous editing, sensitive eye, sense of beauty and form, and skill in bringing this manuscript to a finished stage.

We cannot sufficiently thank our wives, Birgitta Kovalenko and Michelle Thomsen for their unstinting patience and support for this project.

Finally, we want to acknowledge ahead of time those of you who will read this book, apply it to your life, and ultimately improve both your own lives and what we have done here. This is not a finished product, but a stepping stone to something much grander. We look forward to that vision. Thank you, dear reader.

Contents

APPENDIXES

Preface

Have you ever been frustrated by a confusing dream? Have you wondered what it is saying to you? This book can help. THE CREEI PROCESS is a simple and direct guide to understanding the personal meaning of your dreams.

By understanding the simple concepts presented in this book you will open this portal to gain insights into what your dreams mean to you, and help you to follow trends of your dreams through time. Consider it as a doorway between your head and heart. By reflecting on your dreams in the systematic way that THE CREEI PROCESS provides, your waking mind is enabled to explore the feelings and messages they present. Doing this allows your thinking mind to appreciate the inner reality of your dreams and understand the importance of reflecting on them in a systematic way.

Dreams are sometimes troubling, bizarre, and strange, yet other times comforting and calming. Your dream experiences do not obey the usual laws of nature, and so it is easy to dismiss them. Don't dismiss them. Instead, do listen to them by opening that door to meaning and noting your dream-self's behavior. Then ask your dream self twelve easy-to-answer questions and then identify the pattern of your responses. You can then decide what to do with what you have learned. Answering these questions will help you find new meaning.

THE CREEI PROCESS is a practical technique that allows our thinking and feeling functions to be equal partners. We authors intentionally avoid struggling with or debating academic psychological terms like unconscious, subconscious, consciousness, id, ego, superego, right brain, left brain, etc. Instead, we prefer general terms like thinking and feeling, head and heart, or "waking awareness" and "out-of-awareness" as used by Joseph Dillard, to be more practical.

THE CREEI PROCESS is universal in that it is appropriate for anyone regardless of age, race, gender, economic status, education, or cultural background. It does not conflict with any ideology or religion.

Instead it supplements any belief system. This book is for anyone who dreams. That is everyone including you, who wishes to find their meaning. Don't worry if you have a hard time remembering your dreams. We will help you with that.

THE CREEI PROCESS has wide applications. It actually works best when shared with others. We encourage you to talk issues over with a trusted friend, family member, counselor, or clergy. It can be used by counselors and clergy to help their clients clarify issues. A major strength of THE CREEI PROCESS is that you can share your dreams without having to share potentially embarrassing features. It opens new lines of communication.

THIS BOOK IS DESIGNED TO GENTLY EASE YOU INTO THE CONCEPTS NECESSARY TO USE THE CREEI PROCESS. HERE IS HOW IT IS LAID OUT:

PART ONE describes THE CREEI PROCESS.

In CHAPTER 1 you first *experience* it. Your brain will probably object, telling you that you can't possibly do this because you don't understand it completely. Don't be afraid to make mistakes, just do it.

In CHAPTER 2 you will learn more about the twelve questions, be introduced to the scoring system of answering those questions, and also the patterns that the scoring reveals.

CHAPTER 3 will deal with THE CREEI PROCESS in considerable detail. Study it carefully before going on. Actually do the process a few times, maybe as many as ten or more. Give it a try.

PART TWO deals with doing THE CREEI PROCESS as a group.

CHAPTER 4 takes you through some of the barriers people bring to THE CREEI PROCESS.

In CHAPTER 5 you will learn how to teach THE CREEI PROCESS if you want to share it with others.

PART THREE enlarges on the applications of THE CREEI PROCESS.

CHAPTER 6 will look at applying THE CREEI PROCESS to published dreams of people, both real and fictional.

CHAPTER 7 will show how THE CREEI PROCESS can be even more broadly applied than only to your own dreams.

In the **APPENDICES** we present some of our own dreams and how they were scored, dreams from Freud, Jung and Tolstoy. They also include the impact of THE CREEI PROCESS on people, examples of the Integral Deep Listening (IDL) protocols of Joseph Dillard, and finally Eugene Kovalenko's story of the development of THE CREEI PROCESS.

THE CREEI PROCESS is a useful tool. You may not need to know everything about how or why a tool works. You just need an owner's manual and some patience. Use THE CREEI PROCESS as a tool and it will work for you.

Foreword

In the summer of 2017, I was honored to be one of the speakers at the International Association for the Study of Dreams (IASD) in Southern California. One of the perks of being a speaker at the IASD is you get to attend the other seminars, lectures and workshops during the time you're not speaking. As I was flipping through the catalogue to see which dreamwork session I wanted to next attend, I saw a lecture about dreams and shamanism that caught my eye. I took note of the ballroom, and bee-lined on over.

Note: When you attend a dream conference of any kind, especially one sponsored by the IASD, you are consciously and deliberately placing yourself in a vortex outside ordinary reality—a reality the late Rod Serling would've called "The Twilight Zone."

Feeling the "in between realms" energy, I padded carefully into the dark ballroom, and maneuvered to a seat on the right side of the front row. I looked up to see blaring on the screen:

"A Practical Process for Working with the Structure of Dreams: THE CREEI PROCESS, with Eugene N. Kovalenko."

No! Wait a minute? I'm in the wrong room! This isn't the shaman dreaming workshop—in fact, this is the farthest thing from it... because the description read, "In this workshop we will not share out loud about your dreams." That's crazy! Not my style, at all! How can you possibly accomplish anything significant if you don't expose the dream and talk about it... out loud! Dreamwork is revealing, and it's supposed to be. I've got to get out of here!

Just then, a bearded man walked to the front of the room.

Darn! It's starting...it would be rude to leave now...and I'm in the front row. I'll just listen for a few minutes, and as soon as he turns his back, I'll gather my belongings and in a flash of lightning, exit stage right...he won't even know I was here!

His baritone voice lulled me in as he sang the old spiritual "I'm Just a Poor Wayfaring Stranger," and his mischievous eyes twinkled and beguiling smile were so mesmerizing.

He's a trickster...maybe he is the shaman I came here to meet... funny...real shamans would never introduce themselves to you as a shaman...they'd be sneakier than that. Hmm...maybe I'm supposed to be here, after all.

I relaxed in my seat and listened with rapt attention as the bearded mischief maker shared with us his method of dreamwork, which was a million miles from what I was accustomed to. In his CREEI Process, I learned to take a dream, and instead of talking about it, take inventory of it by writing CREEI across the top of a sheet of paper. Each of the letters in CREEI represent categories in which to evaluate your dream. If this seems complicated, don't worry, it's not, and Eugene explains this in detail in the book you are now reading.

The dream I brought into the workshop was, shall we say, traumatic, in an ego-annihilating kind of way. To say the least, it left me feeling off center, angry, and worried. This was a dream that I needed to talk through in order to find resolution...or so I thought.

All I know is that about halfway through the workshop, the light-bulbs began flashing over my head. At first one at a time, and then in rapid succession...so much so, that I began to cry, then laugh, at the same time. As much as I tried to be polite and keep this experience to myself, Eugene took notice.

Sorry to distract from the class, I thought. I'm just bursting with insight about this dream and what it's trying to show me. Your process is amazing!

I was awestruck at the fact that just an hour earlier I'd accidentally walked into a class I didn't want to attend, carrying a burdensome dream I didn't want to admit was mine... and I walked out feeling ten feet tall. I was flooded with gratitude for my blessed mistake, because I was flush with empowerment by THE CREEI PROCESS, my dream... and this amazing bearded man!

Eugene shared with me the many situations where dream details should be kept private. Most people don't realize the extent to which they reveal themselves when they share their dreams. And, unfortunately, there are places and spaces where dream sharing might not work in someone's best interest. So, if you are one of those people who happens to work or live in a situation like this, THE CREEI PROCESS is here so you can still work your dreams, and even have a discussion about them, without having to reveal top secret information about yourself.

After the workshop, I had the blessing of engaging in an impromptu conversation with Eugene, and was mesmerized by his stories and thunderstruck by what a truly remarkable human being he is. His incredible gifts of wisdom, depth and intuition can only be matched by his humor and warmth. I hope you open your heart and mind to experiencing him and his work as I have.

Eugene's CREEI Process is enlightening, grounded and formed by thousands of hours of time-tested research, and is a blessing to all of us who want to take a deeper dive into understanding the mysteries of our dreams and dreaming mind... and still stay somewhat secretive about it.

Enjoy!

Kelly Sullivan Walden (aka "Doctor Dream")

P.S. Because my experience with CREEI was so impactful, I later wrote a poem about the dream that I brought it to the workshop. If you care to see my soul X-ray (aka dream)—clearly, I'm not the secretive type—it's in APPENDIX A at the end of this book. I will caution you, however, it does involve adult language. So, if you are offended by that, just go on and read this book, and omit those pages.

PART ONE

THE CREEI PROCESS

The Twelve Questions

1.   Is the scene clear? Can you describe it, whether
      or not you understand its meaning?

2.   Are you responding to dream characters in a thoughtful
      way rather than reflexively reacting to them?

3.   Is your emotion (passion) high?

4.   Are you fully expressing your emotion?

5.   Are you interacting with others rather
      than withdrawing or absent?

6.   Is the scene complete or resolved?

7.   Is the dream pleasant?

8.   In the dream, do you feel safe?

9.   Do you have a healthy self-esteem or self-worth?

10.   Are you being your authentic present self
      rather than posturing or pretending?

11.   Are you beloving of others in the dream (i.e. relating to other
      dream characters in such a way that they experience their
      own beauty), and in so doing, you experience your own?

12.   Are you becoming all that you can be? That is,
      are you moving toward your highest self?

Chapter 1

CREEI PROCESS QUICKSTART

Here we lay out the concepts quickly. They will make more sense as you work your way through the rest of the book, especially Chapters 2 and 3.

1. Recall a dream, date it the best you can, and assign it a title.

2. Focus on how you are behaving in the dream.

3. Ask your dream self the TWELVE QUESTIONS in order (page 2).

4. Answer each question in one of three simple ways: Yes, No, or Uncertain.

Use a plus sign (+) if it is yes, minus sign (−) if it is no, question mark (?) if you don't know or if you hesitate.

Go ahead. This chapter is intentionally short so you can get a quick feel for what this is about.

Chapter 2

D id you do it, or did you just turn the page? If you just skipped Chapter 1 for whatever reason, please go back and do it. *Experiencing* first is really important.

Now that you have dipped your toes into the water, we authors want to tell a few things about THE CREEI PROCESS itself. Confusion and questions are normal. Just come along on trust for now. **CHAPTER 3** will have much more detail for you.

First, "CREEI" is pronounced like "creek" without the "k." It is an acronym taken from the first letter in the emboldened key words of the first five questions. Why five? Because it is very easy to use your fingers, as shown on the back cover, to go quickly through those first five questions.

The Twelve Questions Again

Now we ask you to do it again, but this time you will get a little more explanation. Think of a recent dream. If you can't think of a dream, choose a life experience, recent or long ago. Answer these questions quickly, yes (+), no (−), or uncertain (?). Be clear that the focus is on you, the dream self in your dream. Don't think too much. If you hesitate, you probably should indicate this hesitation with (?). Don't fret if you don't quite understand the questions; they will become clearer later. These questions have no right or wrong answers.

The Twelve Questions (detail)

1. [C] Is the scene clear? Can you describe the physical setting of the dream and the appearance of the dream characters?

2. [R] Are you thoughtfully responding to dream characters rather than reflexively reacting to them?

3. [E] Is your emotion (passion) high in contrast to no emotion at all? Intense emotion, whether it is extreme fear or perfect love, is the issue.

4. [E] Are you expressing your emotion? There are many different ways to express yourself.

5. [I] Are you interacting with others rather than withdrawing or being absent? This is similar to the last question but focuses more on action rather than emotion.

6. [C] Is the scene complete, resolved or fulfilling? We are looking for a sense of closure.

7. [P] Is the dream pleasant?

8. [S] In the dream do you feel safe?

9. [E] Do you have a healthy self-esteem?

10. [A] Are you being your authentic self rather than posturing or pretending? We are looking for your level of honesty with other dream characters and with yourself.

11. [B] Are you beloving of others in the dream? That is, are you relating to other dream characters in such a way that they experience their own beauty?

12. [B] Are you becoming all that you can be? We look to see if you are moving toward your highest self, the best you are capable of.

Look at these questions. None of them asks you about the content or the "meaning" of your dream. Now just think for a bit about what the answers to these questions might be telling you about yourself. You may be pretty confused by now, but it will all be much clearer in the next chapter.

Recording the Scores

If you keep a dream journal, first give the dream a one or two word title and record both the date of the dream and the date you score it. Then write out the dream using the present tense. This gives a greater immediacy in the experience of telling the dream story.

Next, score your dream by recording in the shorthand form with a double forward slashes between questions five and six and also between questions eight and nine. For example, for a pattern where all questions are answered "yes" or (+) write: **+++++//+++//++++**. You will see this notation throughout this book. Place this scoring directly beneath the dream in your dream notebook if you keep one.

CREEI Patterns

Four CREEI patterns guide you on what you might do with the information in the dream as discussed later in Chapter Three. See if they work for you, and if not, then feel free to come up with new ones that are more practical. If you do please share them with us. Your insights are welcome.

The four patterns are TRANSFORMATIVE (pattern 1), MOTIVATIONAL (pattern 2), ANTICIPATORY (pattern 3), and TRAUMATIC (pattern 4).

TRANSFORMATIVE. If all of the questions are answered (+) the dream is considered transformative, comforting, or confirming. This is a rare pattern, but when it happens it often carries such a clear personal message for you that you are likely never to forget.

MOTIVATIONAL. If only one or two questions are answered with a (−) or (?). Because it is so close to a TRANSFORMATIVE pattern that it may motivate you with only a little effort to realize what it would take to have made it TRANSFORMATIVE. For example, if the "non (+)" answer is to the sixth question (completion), you might consider how to make the story in your waking mind come to resolution. The motivational dream is the ideal pattern for experiencing the creative process. You will see how this works in **CHAPTER 3**.

ANTICIPATORY. When three or more of the first six questions are scored as (−) or (?), this kind of dream often suggests that something may be coming that you are not aware of. When this happens, remember the images and be prepared for what may yet be manifested in the outer world.

TRAUMATIC. When three or more of the last six questions score (−) or (?), this frequently indicates that you may be suffering with some kind of burden. If so, do not carry it alone. Work with someone that you trust, whether a professional, group, clergy, or trusted friend. Joseph Dillard's Integral Deep Listening (IDL) protocol is ideal for interpreting and dealing with such patterns.[1]

Some dreams score with a combination of patterns. The most common combination is ANTICIPATORY and TRAUMATIC. This double pattern is typical of the dreams of first-time CREEI workshop and seminar participants. Some dreams have elements of other patterns. How they are labeled is not as important as the insights you gain by answering the questions simply and reflecting on your (−) and (?) answers.

Tracking Dreams Using Spreadsheets

Once the dream is scored you may want to transfer the score to a CREEI scan spreadsheet as shown in **Spreadsheet 1**. There are sections for date and title of the dream, answers to each of the questions, notations on two of the most important dream characters, and the pattern.

---

[1] See **APPENDIX F.**

Throughout this book we spell out the dream pattern, but the short hand numbers work better on the spreadsheet. For example use "3,4" instead of "ANTICIPATORY-TRAUMATIC" in the "Ptn" column, as illustrated in the Cumulative CREEI scan spreadsheet in **Spreadsheet 1**.

Tracking the pattern trends in dreams will allow you to follow your emotional development more easily. For example, have your dreams been more or less pleasant with time? If your dreams are becoming less pleasant, it may be a warning signal to you that conditions around you have been changing and you need to pay special attention. You can see that trend more easily on a spreadsheet.

The written spreadsheet is fine, especially for individual use, but using a computerized spreadsheet program like Excel or Numbers gives greater flexibility in sorting dreams according to dreamer, date, or dream pattern. **Spreadsheets 2a** and **2b** in CHAPTER 4 show how the program separated out the dreams of two of the participants in a CREEI seminar.

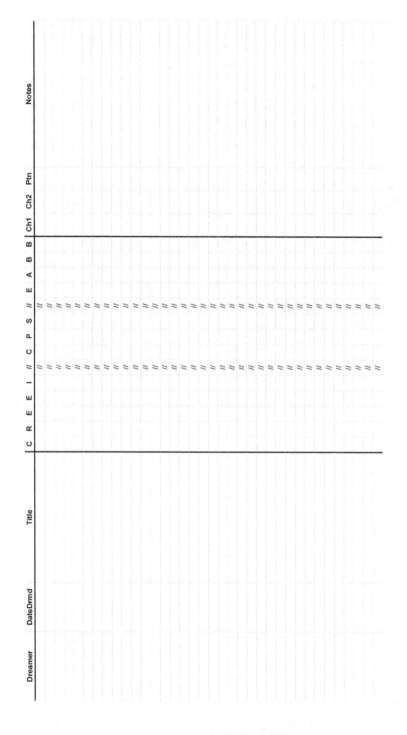

Spreadsheet 1. Blank Template for Cumulative CREEI Scores.

Chapter 3

HOW THE CREEI PROCESS WORKS

This chapter details how THE CREEI PROCESS works by asking the twelve questions, scoring the answers, and noting the patterns they may represent. The first step on this deeper exploration is to identify explicitly the assumptions that underlie the process.

CREEI Assumptions

Every process rests on basic assumptions or principles. Those underlying THE CREEI PROCESS need to be understood and acknowledged if it is to be used effectively. Without knowing the basics it is easy to get ambushed in THE CREEI PROCESS. We will enlarge on each. Here are the assumptions:

Dreaming is a universal human experience

Dreaming goes beyond culture, society, language, age, race, or any other way we categorize people.[2] Some people deny they dream, but experience shows that they simply have a harder time remembering their dreams. The next chapter has suggestions for getting through this problem. Everyone dreams, and so THE CREEI PROCESS can be applied by everyone.

---

[2] In fact it goes beyond species. If you have ever watched a sleeping dog chasing a rabbit, you know that they dream too.

Dreams are pictures of feelings that reflect waking life

Feelings come from the heart rather than from the head. The dream characters, animate or inanimate, are images that clothe the emotional message.

Dreams are personal metaphors

Only the dreamer is the ultimate interpretive authority. No one else can tell you what it means. They may say, "If it were my dream, here is how I would interpret it," but they may not impose that interpretation. You are free to agree or reject their interpretation. Dreams present images and dramas of deeper personal truths, but only the dreamer can say what truths they tell.

Each dream always contains new information

Even recurring dreams are never identical. We can generally recognize differences in repeating dreams, and those differences hold the key to their deeper meaning. It is your feeling self that keeps trying to get through to your thinking self by presenting the repeating message from different angles.

There is no such thing as a meaningless dream

All dreams are a communication from heart to waking awareness and so deserve attention. Some may have more immediate impact than others, and some will have impact months or years later.

Even the tiniest fragment is important. A brief flash of a dream is as important as the most vivid and prolonged dream whether we understand them at the time or not. Consider the grain of sand in the famous poem by William Blake,[3] *Auguries of Innocence,* that begins:

> To see a World in a Grain of Sand
> And Heaven in a Wild Flower,
> Hold Infinity in the palm of your hand
> And Eternity in an hour.

The CREEI Process may be applied to any event, whether dreaming or waking

This point will be expanded in CHAPTER 8. Dreams are the most obvious application of THE CREEI PROCESS, once mastered it is useful to apply to many other experiences in life where heart and head go hand in hand.

In The CREEI Process dream content need not be disclosed

This is an important safety mechanism. It is crucial and perhaps the most important contribution of CREEI. We can talk about a dream without discussing its content and still get value from it. Perhaps the content of a dream is embarrassing to you. You can still talk about the dream in terms of its CREEI score without embarrassment or revealing classified information.

The CREEI Process is non-interpretive

"Interpretation" is the process of examining the dream contents and explaining what they mean. THE CREEI PROCESS analyzes by asking questions of the structure of the dream but does not tell the dreamer what it means. Further explanation is left to the dreamer.

---

[3] https://www.poetryloverspage.com/poets/blake/to_see_world.html

The CREEI Process is objective rather than subjective

Once a dream is written down, applying the questions should score similarly or identically whether scored by the dreamer or another person. We have learned during many workshops and seminars that there is fairly uniform agreement on how to score the written dreams of others. This is not always so, but some of the most interesting understandings emerge when there are disagreements in scoring. The scoring is subjective but when written down becomes an objective tool for discussion of individual dreams and comparisons of an individual's different dreams through time.

The CREEI Process is non-judgmental

Regardless of the pattern of the dream, THE CREEI PROCESS does not pass judgment on the dream as good or bad. It just is.

Dreams bypass the control of our thinking self

Our thinking self typically considers itself to be in control and works hard to keep it that way. The heart synthesizes experiences in a different way than the head does, but has no language other than dreams or emotions to communicate its message. The dream is a story that tells the heart's truth.

Peace and joy exist or can be found in any dream

This is without a doubt the most debated and contested point at dream workshops. No matter how disturbing or unpleasant a dream is, when you learn its wisdom by answering the TWELVE QUESTIONS you may hear its message more clearly and experience how it has the power to transform you.[4]

---

[4] See Joseph Dillard's IDL protocols in APPENDIX F.

Writing your Dreams

Most dreams are quickly forgotten unless you work at remembering them. When you have awakened, jot some key words in a notebook you keep by your bed. These are important to help you get back into the dream. Later, as soon as you get a chance write the story out. This is best in a dream journal where all your dreams are together. Write just one dream per page if you can, so that you can write notes later as you understand the dream better. Writing the dream out in long-hand gives your brain time to remember the details better than if you are dictating to a voice-recognition program or typing on the computer. As you write, small details from the dream will typically flood back to you as you re-live the dream.

Be sure to write in the present tense, such as "I am walking through a bright forest," rather than "I walked through a bright forest." This helps you to capture the freshness of the dream, and it helps to remember details, some of which are crucial to your self-understanding later. In writing this way, you re-experience the dream in real time, but now in your waking awareness. Write in first person, like "I am turning on the windshield wipers." This helps with the CREEI scoring, too. Look at how Bob struggled with dreams from Tolstoy's War and Peace, presented in Appendix D until Bob transformed them into first person.

You may realize as you write that there are sudden scene shifts, even though it seems like the same dream. These multi-scene dreams are best scored separately, as if each scene was a stand-alone dream. As the scores differ from scene to scene, you may become aware of trends within the dream that help your understanding.

At the end of the write-up, list the characters in the dream besides you as the dream self. Characters are animate or inanimate, but are still characters. If you dream that Aunt Millie has appeared to you wearing her apron, shaking her mixing spoon at you, and telling you that you are condemned to eternal perdition if you smoke the cigarette she found you holding, then Aunt Millie, apron, mixing spoon, and cigarette are all characters. Begin with the assumption that every dream character is an expression of some aspect of yourself. So it isn't really Aunt Millie coming to visit you, it is part of you. Don't blame poor Aunt Millie, herself. Realizing this will help you to take responsibility for your own experience and grow from it. You may learn a lot by observing how she, as a given dream character, functions in each of your dreams. Watch how your perception evolves and gain valuable insights into who you are.

CREEI Questions in Detail

As you answer the questions don't over-think your responses. You can always reconsider your scoring as you learn more about the dream. Remember that just because a question is scored (–) does not mean that it is unhelpful or bad. These actually may be the most valuable questions to reflect on and learn from. THE CREEI PROCESS is intended to detect one's state of intra-personal balance. The (–) and (?) answers allow you to focus on self-aspects that are out of balance. If any answers give you an "aha" feeling, that is "gold" and worth remembering.

C—CLARITY. Is the dream clear? Can you describe it whether or not you understand it?
+ if the dream is clear, direct and undistorted
? if the dream is vague and only somewhat describable
– if the dream is confused or indistinct

When you are able to describe the story of the dream in words, you should score it as a (+). This does not necessarily mean that you understand the dream, only that you can describe what is happening. Not all of the details of the dream need to be completely clear. You don't need every detail of the events, contexts, locales, or identities of people or other dream characters to call it clear.

For example, if you dream of a fish, you may know that it is definitely a fish, and a fish of generally a given size, but maybe you can't describe the fish in all of its details or identify what kind of fish it is. That is okay. It does not matter if it is a valuable fish or a poisonous fish or has other kinds of elements or aspects or meanings to it. You just need to be able to say it was a fish rather than a rabbit or stone. The details may give more meaning, but do not need to be there for it to be clear.

Some dreams are purely sounds where you can't see any images. Perhaps the dream is a voice or a song. If the sounds are clear, the dream is clear. Clear dreams tend to be more memorable, but that is not a judgment on their importance. Unclear dreams are sometimes the most unsettling but at the same time instructive. Those are important dreams even if they are not comfortable or calming.

R—RESPONSIVENESS[5]. Are you being responsive or proactive in the dream? Are you responding constructively rather than reflexively reacting?

+   if you are fully active and responsive
?   if you have difficulty telling the difference between being responsive or reactive
−   if you are reactive in a knee-jerk fashion

The question has to do with how thoughtful you as the dream self are being in your actions that you do because of the actions of other dream characters. Responding is considering the circumstances and acting wisely whereas reacting is simply doing on impulse what you always do even if that leads to destructive results.

E—EMOTION. Are you experiencing emotion in the dream?

+   if your emotion is high
?   if your emotion is moderate or questionable
−   if you have little, low, or no emotion

This question asks about the intensity of your emotional experience in the dream, regardless of its quality. It looks at the contrast between being emotional versus having no emotional response at all.

---

[5] "Respondability" is another "R" word. Although it is not in the dictionary, it may nevertheless help you tell the difference between responding and reacting.

One can have strong emotions while watching a movie, for example, without being able to change anything on the screen. Interactions and involvements in the activities of the dream are not at issue in this question. For the technically minded, this could be compared to "voltage" or "potential energy."

E—EXPRESSION. Are you as the dream-self fully expressing your emotions?

+   if you are fully expressing yourself in the dream
?   if you are only moderately expressing your emotions
-   if you are not expressing your emotions at all

You may have high emotion, as described in the last question, but unable to communicate it. For example, you may be witnessing a burning building in which you see a child at the window. This would usually provoke in you as the dream-self a strong emotion, in which you would be motivated to shout out to the firefighter about the situation, or start to cry, or to rush into the building to save the child yourself, or you may even run away. Those are all expressions of how you feel. For the technically minded this could be compared to electrical current, "amperage" or "kinetic energy." Of course if you are not emotional at all or can't tell if you have emotion, you can hardly expect to be able to express it. In technical terms this could be considered as having high resistance or being insular.

I—INTERACTION. Are you interacting or converging with other dream characters rather than withdrawing or being alone? Are you speaking with or doing things with other characters in the dream (in either a positive or negative way)?

+   if you are involved with other characters (coming toward other dream characters in some converging way)

?   if you have only moderate involvement

−   if you have little or no contact (moving away or isolating), or are an out-side observer

This is sometimes hard to separate from the last question, although it is certainly possible to interact with others whether or not you are expressing your feelings.

C—COMPLETION. Is the scene complete or resolved? Is there a sense of closure or resolution?

+   if you feel the dream is fully telling its story

?   if you feel the possibility of some resolution but are not sure

−   if you feel the dream is neither complete nor resolved

Have the loose ends of the dream story been resolved? Without completion, a situation will remain without a satisfactory ending. Most dreams seem not to have a sense of completion. Something happens to shift the dream to a new scene, or often to wake you up ending the dream. In Chapter 4 you in your waking state will learn how to creatively convert a (−) to a (+) and find completion.

P—PLEASANTNESS. Was it a pleasing dream?

+   if you are comfortable and in a pleasing situation

?   if you are in neither a pleasant nor unpleasant situation

−   if you are in an unpleasant or uncomfortable situation

It is not necessary to over-analyze this question. If the dream was an experience you would like to have again, a comfortable situation, a scenario where you feel joy and/or beauty, then score the dream as (+).

S—SAFETY. Do you feel safe?

+ if you feel safe and confident
? if you feel neither safe nor fearful
- if you feel unsafe or fearful

This is usually obvious and does not need belaboring. Judge how threatened you may feel by the other dream characters or situations. Is someone pointing a loaded gun at you? Are you tottering at the edge of a cliff? Is a tornado about to sweep you away? Are you being threatened by financial problems or lawsuits? All of these situations obviously score unsafe. However, you may be in a chaotic situation with violence and danger all around, but nevertheless feel that you are in a bubble, isolated from all of that. If none of those threatening situations could affect you, then you should score it as (+). You as the dream-self were safe even if other dream characters were not.

E—ESTEEM. Do you, as the dream-self, feel that your interactions with other dream characters reflect a healthy self-esteem or self-worth?

+ if you feel self-confident
? if you are unsure of yourself
- if your self-worth is low

Other positive ways of asking this are: Are you proud of what you are doing, do you approve of yourself as acting within your own set of values, or do you feel good about yourself? Low self-esteem may involve emotions of shame or fear. This question does not address whether anyone else in the world agrees with you, only how you feel in the dream.

A—AUTHENTICITY. Are you behaving genuinely without pretending or posturing?

+   if you are being authentic
?   if you are not sure
−   if you are pretending or posturing to be something other than who you really are

This question does not address whether you think you are is a good person or bad person. This can get us into the large area of sin and transgressions at a moral level, far beyond the scope of this book. A dream in which you are behaving contrary to what you perceive to be your guiding moral compass may very well yield rich self-insights. Perhaps you feel you are not being authentic in the dream and suddenly become aware of situations in your waking life where you were behaving in the same way.

B—BELOVING. Are other dream characters experiencing their beauty in your presence?

+   if you are participating with others in the dream in such a way that they experience their own beauty
?   if you are neither helping others nor trying to be dominant
−   if you are trying to achieve dominance over others (i.e., power-tripping)

Beloving depends on the experience of the other dream characters in your presence, not your experience of them. It is the action of spending time or interacting with other dream characters (animate or inanimate) in such a way that the character experiences his, her, or its own beauty.

When Eugene first learned and comprehended the word *beloving* in the early '90s as he learned it from Prof. Mac Freeman of Queens College in Kingston, Canada, he was greatly affected. Mac taught what he called the "Five Bs," which were "Beloving, Becoming, Beholding, Believing and Belonging." Eugene immediately added them all to THE CREEI PROCESS, which was then still under development. Although the last three B word questions were eventually dropped,

Eugene realized the unique importance of Mac's definition of beloving after he found it so convicting and painful to begin with, but then surprisingly liberating.

The Oxford English Dictionary defines "beloving" simply as "loving." We are using it in a somewhat different way where the important thing is not your behavior in the dream but rather how the dream characters experience your behavior.

This concept may be easier to understand by asking the opposite meaning, which is "power tripping" or being narcissistic and unconcerned about the welfare or experience of others. You may not even be aware of your unconcern for others, and answering this question honestly creates a great opportunity for self-assessment as you reflect on and score the dream.

B—BECOMING. Are you, as the dream self, moving in a direction toward all that you can be, or more of who you are capable of being?

- **+**   if you have a sense of being joyfully yourself
- **?**   if you are hiding from or avoiding others or circumstances
- **−**   if you are procrastinating or putting off until later the actions that need to be done

Do you have a sense of being happy with yourself or that what you are doing brings you joy? Are you moving toward your highest self? The opposite of becoming is procrastinating, being in a rut or putting off efforts at personal growth.

Of all the twelve CREEI questions, Becoming asks how well you are fulfilling the needs outlined by Maslow's pyramid of human needs.[6] At the base are security and safety. Built on that foundation are our psychological needs such as elevation of esteem, then our need for belonging in relationships. At the apex is achieving our full potential,

---

[6] https://psychclassics.yorku.ca/Maslow/motivation.htm. See A. H. Maslow. A Theory of Human Motivation. Originally Published in Psychological Review, 50, 370-396 (1943)

our becoming. Positive responses to the CREEI questions mean that many of our greatest human needs are being met.

Review of the Four CREEI Patterns

1. TRANSFORMATIVE:
   All yes (**+**)
   +++++//+++//++++

2. MOTIVATIONAL:
   Only one or two no's (**−**) or uncertain (**?**)
   +−+++//+++//++++, or
   +−+++//+++//+?++

3. ANTICIPATORY:
   Three or more (**−**) or (**?**) in the first six questions
   +−+−+//?++//++++

4. TRAUMATIC:
   Three or more (**−**) or (**?**) in the last six questions
   +++++//+−?//−+??

A good way to learn scoring and patterns is to see how it is done. More dreams examples are provided in APPENDIX B to show how the authors have scored and patterned some of their own dreams. They are copied without changes from their dream journals, followed by their scoring and why we authors scored them in that way. Discussions of how to work with these patterns are presented in the next section.

Working with Your Dreams

Now having learned how to apply THE CREEI PROCESS to your dream, you are ready to use the tool to understand what your feeling self is expressing. The ultimate aim is to figure out how the dream could be re-imagined to become a Transformative dream. Whether your dreams are comforting or terrifying, the effort you put in to understand their messages will ultimately be a significantly positive influence in your life. Allow your conscious actions to be informed by what you learn from your dreams. Threats often transform when their messages are heard and understood. Learn to appreciate ambiguities, multiple meanings, and the many subtle shades between black-and-white issues. Working with a dream will often bring great rewards, but sometimes it takes wrestling with it several times.

What you do with a dream will vary greatly depending on the type of dream and its contents. Recognizing the dream pattern will guide you. Look especially at the (−) and (?) answers and imagine how you would create satisfactory resolutions to unsatisfying and/or incomplete dreams. Don't be afraid of playing with a dream or of letting it sit for a while. If you have written it down, you can always come back to it later when it makes more sense to you.

TREASURING A TRANSFORMATIVE DREAM

Remembering a TRANSFORMATIVE dream can bring untold joy and comfort to your waking self. Treasure it. Maybe even share it. Such dreams typically carry an important personal message. You may relive the dream whenever you choose and can always return to it at any time for joy, confirming and comfort.

WORKING WITH A MOTIVATIONAL DREAM

MOTIVATIONAL dreams are ideally suited for dream work since it takes only one or two imagined yes's (+) to bring them to TRANSFORMATIVE. In working with your dreams your waking self is trying to improve the dream in whatever areas it is lacking. You want to see how you as the dream self could have behaved in the dream to achieve a (+) score in each question.

Any creative activity is appropriate for MOTIVATIONAL dreams. You may want to do a drawing or painting, a sculpture, a dance, a mathematical equation, or a piece of music. Poetry has been especially useful. Do not be intimidated by feeling you have no skills in these creative areas. This is a door opening to the creative process.

As an example, here is a suggestion for writing a poem to modify your dream. This has worked well for some CREEI Process participants. Rewrite the dream as a poem in three stanzas: (a) objective stanza. (b) subjective stanza, (c) TRANSFORMATIVE stanza. In the first stanza rewrite the dream using key words such that it scores the same as your dream. Concentrate on distilling what may be a lot of verbiage into something simple. In the second stanza there are no rules. You can do anything you want in it. For example, you can say (to yourself) "I don't like this dream" or "I object to its content" in expressing yourself in this stanza. Also, feel free to invite new dream characters in to help you, even if they were not in the dream in the first place. For example, you can invite "Jesus" or any heroes you can imagine. The only limit is your imagination. Just start messing with it. It can score any way you want. In the third stanza rewrite the dream such that it scores TRANS-FORMATIVE. This stanza is usually the hardest to write, but in doing this, you should experience a sense of satisfaction, resolution or joy. It can be a lot of hard, emotional work but is well worth the effort.

Here is an example.

Bob

LEARNING RELATIONSHIPS, September 21, 2017
*I am at a lecture of some sort with other
people. It is about spiritual subjects. The first
speaker is a woman about forty years old who is
telling us about relationships and how to make
deep relationships. She comes around to each of us
and touches us gently to demonstrate how to do it.
It is very nice to learn.*

CREEI SCORE: . . . . . **+++++//−++//++++**
MOTIVATIONAL

I scored (–) for completion (12 Questions #6) because I did not feel that I was able to use what she had taught me to actually make deep relationships, so the experience felt incomplete. Here is the poem that I wrote.

FROM DREAM TO POEM

I felt her touch, her fingers on my shoulder
Were light and gentle, reaching deep to my core
I want to reach out, touch deeply,
As she had, but can I?

What hell it would be
To never touch or be touched,
To never feel the pressure
Of another's hand.
We speak with our touch
To the core of another, our voice.

I felt her touch, her fingers on my shoulder
Were light and gentle, and I found myself
Turning, touching the shoulders of my neighbors
My touch told how deeply I loved them.

This may not be great poetry, but the first stanza reflects the dream. The second stanza talks about how important touch is, and the third stanza, I think, resolves the issue by practicing the precious skill of touching deeply.

WORKING WITH TRAUMATIC OR ANTICIPATORY DREAMS

TRAUMATIC and ANTICIPATORY dreams often linger for days or years. If it troubles you don't carry the burden of these kinds of dreams alone. Just talking through a dream with a trusted friend can help you see how you can transform yourself to a healthier state of being. Once you have become comfortable with creative activities like poetry for MOTIVATIONAL dreams, you may want to try it for ANTICIPATORY patterns. But it is best not used for TRAUMATIC patterns. Advanced techniques such as Joseph Dillard's Integral Deep Listening (IDL) mentioned in APPENDIX F, or Carl Jung's active imagination methodology[7] are helpful, especially if you are already experienced with dream work.

Here is an example from Eugene's dream work with an ANTICIPATORY-TRAUMATIC dream. This was about a decade before he developed THE CREEI PROCESS and before he developed the three-stanza poem presented before.

Eugene
ABOUT TO BE FIRED, January 1, 1978
At the time of this dream, I was living by myself in a small garage apartment and working for an engineering company.

I am at a meeting, sitting in the front row on the left side, three chairs from the aisle. An executive for the company I work for comes over to me and demands to know what I have been doing. He warns that I am about to be fired, but I don't know what I have done.

That is when I wake up.

CREEI SCORE: . . . . . **+?+-?//---//??-?**
ANTICIPATORY-TRAUMATIC

Eugene explains: "At the time of this New Year's Day dream, Southern California was experiencing an historic drought, and all reservoirs were at dangerously low levels. I was startled by the content of the dream and didn't know what to think about it. However, three days later, I had a back spasm before going to work and couldn't even get up. Having called to work to report being ill, I had time to read. One book I happened to have contained stories that Jung and others told about rainmakers in China, how they were invited to go to certain places in the country that were suffering drought and what they did

---

[7] https://medium.com/@SteafanFox/carl-jungs-active-imagination-technique-2a622e00311

about it. That is what inspired this poem, the idea of what a rainmaker does. As I worked on putting this poem into poetic form, it actually began to rain! It was a huge storm, which filled up all the reservoirs, essentially breaking the drought. It was spooky! Here is the first version of the poem I wrote three days after the dream."

RAINMAKER

I'm nervous as I sit in front
The third chair from the aisle.
The man who sits before me
Now speaks but doesn't smile.

"What is your journey here, sir?
Before you are retired,
And make no joke about it
The word is more like fired!"

Startled, I woke that New Year's Day
As the dream began to fade,
And three days later on the job
My back just up and gave!

Down flat in bed my body lay
Retired by the pain
While outside great clouds gathered
And then began the rain.

As outer ragged darkness
Sent torrents raging down
I dimly came to be aware
The Master was in town.

His inner light began to glow
In a schoolroom way down deep
To show me what I'd failed to learn
Long formal years asleep.

He came now as a rainmaker
From regions far away
Where Nature's master rhythm
Is balanced night and day.

He took confusion on himself
Influenced from without
And as the inner struggle grew
Began to sort it out.

A rainmaker comes for inner work
Chaotic states to feel
And restoring balance in himself
New harmony forms congeal.

CREEI Score: . . . . . **+?+−?//−−−//??−?**
Anticipatory-Traumatic

This poem scores the same as the dream.

Eugene continues, "I felt a relationship between the nightmare and my incapacitating back problem, which gave me time to study, and the subsequent life-replenishing rain. I continued to mull over the dream in my mind and decided to write again. The second version was written a month later as I worked with the inner meaning of the dream. As I revisited the poem, I found a profound new sense of self and purpose. The inner company manager character, who so much intimidated me, had now lost his power as I reworked the poem to a satisfying ending."

RAINMAKER (Second stanza and reworked version)

"This is now my journey, Sir,"
I say back in the dream,
"To seek that place where rainmakers
Can learn the craft they bring.

"I know it isn't far beyond
For I can see the way;
The longer are the strides I take
The sooner arrival day.

"Even detours to the right or left
Are harder now to take
As my journey speed increases
It's less effort moving straight.

"So that is where I'm going now,
I hope you understand.
If not, that's all right too, Sir,
But I'm moving to new land.

"I'll return a later time then
When I've better learned my craft,
And if you're here and still in need,
My work will make you laugh.

"If it isn't fun to work here
Anxiously building your careers,
Why work to frantic sweat and toil
If you're always in arrears?

"Send for yourselves a rainmaker.
I know there's one around
Who'll better help than I can give
When invited to your ground."

A rainmaker comes for inner work
Chaotic states to feel
And restoring balance in himself
New harmony forms congeal.

CREEI SCORE: . . . . . **++++//+++//++++**

TRANSFORMATIVE

By reworking the dream through his poetry, Eugene transformed the dream to a genuinely positive experience.

Another example of how this worked well in the hands of a person experienced in considering dreams is the poem in the afterword written by Kelly Sullivan Walden. With one poem she transformed her ANTICIPATORY-TRAUMATIC dream into a TRANSFORMATIVE one.

OLD DREAMS, REPEATING DREAMS, NIGHTMARES, AND LUCID DREAMING

Old Dreams can have new and surprising meanings. A vivid example of this presented in APPENDIX G is a dream Eugene had when in graduate school, "Lucifer Is Here!" More than thirty years later he went back to that first dream and applied THE CREEI PROCESS. Then he applied Joseph Dillard's IDL process to that dream (see APPENDIX F).

Repeating dreams deserve special consideration since participants at dream workshops frequently ask about them. These are the dreams where you can't find your locker at school or forgot to go to a certain class and it is the end of the semester. A repeating dream is your heart calling to you about something troubling. It is wise to pay attention to this and consider it as a wakeup call. The most useful elements to look for in a series of repeating dreams are the differences between the dreams since each dream will nevertheless be a little different. The differences hold the real message. Once those differences are found, they usually point to a resolution and the dream will likely never be dreamed again.

Nightmares are menacing dreams that are often repeating. They can leave a person feeling incapacitated for a long time. Joseph Dillard[8] and Arnold Mindell[9] have done remarkable work in helping people face and understand nightmares.

Nightmares are a frequent feature of post-traumatic stress disorder (PTSD). Eugene has recently done CREEI workshops in

---

[8] Joseph Dillard, https://www.dreamyoga.com/
[9] Arnold Mindell, https://www.aamindell.net/process-work/

his community with military veterans who have been suffering from PTSD. The participants have been uniformly enthusiastic about how THE CREEI PROCESS has helped them to talk about their nightmares without necessarily disclosing all the details of the dreams.

A good app to find on your smart phone that refers to PTSD and nightmares and is called Dream EZ. It is based on work done in the United States Army that indicated that simply telling the dream to another person might make the dream less troubling each time it is dreamed and told.[10]

Lucid Dreaming happens when dreamers are aware they are dreaming. It can be in the middle of a dream or at the end. When it is at the conclusion of a dream, it is a natural transition to the waking state, and this sometimes brings with it relief that the frightening moments being lived in a dream do not have physical reality in the outside world.

Drifting back to sleep and resuming the dream is fine. In this situation, a lucid dreamer continues to listen to the out-of-awareness self but may or may not respect its message. Lucid dreamers might find it useful to quickly review their respective behaviors in their dreams via the CREEI questions *before* making any changes in their lucid dream.

Some years ago Eugene was in communication with a group of young lucid dreamers who were newly learning how to achieve lucidity. He suggested that these new lucid dreamers might consider inventorying themselves via THE CREEI PROCESS while in the lucid state to avoid changing things too soon. They seemed pleased by this suggestion. We feel that the true function of a dream is to convey an important message and if a lucid dreamer attempts to change the dream before understanding this message, the dreamer risks dishonoring the dream and missing what may be an important insight.

---

[10] Personal Communication, Karl "Skip" O. Moe, PhD, Uniformed Services University of the Health Sciences, Bethesda, MD with Robert Thomsen May 2017.

PART TWO

GROUP APPLICATIONS OF THE CREEI PROCESS

Chapter 4

CREEI WORKSHOPS AND SEMINARS

C REEI Workshops are usually done for groups of four to ten people with three to four hour sessions in which the attendees learn how to do THE CREEI PROCESS. The book you are reading can be regarded as a substitute for a workshop.[11] A Seminar is the follow-up for the initial workshop attendees which have two-hour sessions held weekly for an agreed time period of typically six to eight weeks.

Groups interested in THE CREEI PROCESS can assemble for any number of reasons. They may be made up of participants of like-minded community members, church members, members of businesses, military veteran organizations, book clubs, support groups, or people who are just interested in dreams. Unless they are present by court order or their job depends on it, participants generally attend because they want to understand how THE CREEI PROCESS works and what it can do for them.

At the same time they learn more about the others in the group as individuals and as a dynamic group as a whole. CREEI is a quick way for people, whether strangers or those who think they already know each other, to establish not only deep community, but also deeper relationships. Using CREEI, a group of any size and makeup can quickly identify where its problems might be.[12] Through CREEI, participants learn to know their own strengths and weaknesses as well those of other group members, and the group as a whole. The group learns how to work together as a team. THE CREEI PROCESS provides a

---

[11] If you want to see how Eugene conducts a workshop see "CREEI Dream Workshop Parts One and Two" on You Tube from the June 2017 meeting of the International Association for the Study of Dreams.

[12] See Eugene's workshop "Sedona Surprise" in **APPENDIX G.**

structure that invites participants to work with their inner selves and simultaneously with their co-workers in an attitude of inner and outer partnering. This inevitably allows the group to achieve higher morale, creativity and greater meaning.

Barriers People Bring to CREEI Workshops

Frequently, when people come to a CREEI Workshop they bring several levels of resistance to the process. Unfortunately, some people are coerced to be there by a spouse or parent, or because their job depends on it, or some other source of peer pressure. Dealing with these situations in a non-confrontational way helps to bypass these barriers and leads to the probability of success.

Even for those who attend voluntarily, the current culture has so deeply been instilled with the attitude that the thinking mind is the best way to make good decisions. However, CREEI offers a more effective way of making good decisions than solely relying on the head.

Most of the following objections can be defused by enthusiastic group interactions as participants learn how well THE CREEI PROCESS works for them. Let's look at some specific points of resistance and how to deal with them.

"I don't dream."

In **CHAPTER 3**, one of the assumptions is that dreaming is a universal human experience. For a total of about two and a half hours during each night, we all dream in short segments called REM (rapid eye movement) sleep.[13] This is true regardless of age or culture. Dreaming is a daily miracle and a universal human language.

---

[13] See books by Hopson.

"I can't remember my dreams."

The brain seems to have a built-in amnesia about dreams so they are soon forgotten when we awake. They evaporate from our memory like disappearing mist in the morning. We say unequivocally that you will remember your dreams if you want to. The intention is crucial. And if you want to, several techniques will help you enhance dream recall. Naturally, good sleep hygiene is crucial to both having and remembering dreams. Establishing a regular routine for your sleep time will help with this. Avoid sedatives and alcohol near bedtime, as they interfere with the normal sleep cycles. Wind down the evening before going to bed so that your body is ready for the blessings of sleep. Avoid having a radio or podcasts playing in your ears when you sleep.

Again, the intention of remembering dreams is crucial to dream recall. Jan Bayliss suggested doing an auto-suggestion technique as you are going to sleep by repeating ten times a promise to yourself like: "When I wake up, I will remember my dreams vividly and will write them down."

Have a pen and notepad at your bedside. This is useful, and it also reinforces the idea that you take this seriously and that it is important to you. When you awake, lie quietly for a short time and immediately review your dreams for their content so that they are firmly planted in your waking awareness. Then reach for your pen and notepad and write a few words that will remind you of the dream. Later follow the advice in **CHAPTER 3** about writing the dream.[14]

"Dreams aren't scientific."

This attitude asserts that dreams can't be scientifically verified or studied and so are not valid. In fact, there is a large body of knowledge being generated by scientists about dreams.[15] However, the physiology

---

[14] See Bayliss for other suggestions.

[15] See the International Association for the Study Dreams (www.asdreams.org) for one example.

of sleep and dreams, as well as the phenomenon of dreaming itself, is beyond the scope of this how-to book.[16]

Even scientists who have religious faith are often resistant to understanding, or even acknowledging, the out-of-awareness self. Brain, mind and spirit are different, but have not, until recently, been subject to scientific scrutiny. Scientific understanding generally demands repeated, consistent results to fit a theory, and so does religious faith.

CREEI was developed by a PhD scientist/engineer. Outside of a formal academic field of psychology, these data can be charted and followed using standard engineering method. It converts highly subjective materials (dream contents) into objective (empirical) data, which can be charted and followed in spreadsheets (see **Spreadsheet 1**). Although dreams aren't subject to standard scientific proof, CREEI is an effective tool to study their empirical reality.

"It was just a dream."

A skeptical participant in one of the early workshops said, "Dreams are merely random firings of my brain when I am asleep and hold no meaning for me." End of discussion. No need to go further. That was before he had an extraordinary experience in the follow-up seminar. In any case, this attitude flies in the face of ideas embraced by a large body of professional psychologists and psychiatrists who feel we make a major mistake to marginalize dreams. Dreaming is a subject of the ever-growing science of understanding the sleep process and the role that sleep plays in our general health. You will know that dreams are important when you experience their impact on you. That influence, even if it is a nightmare, is made positive by honest efforts to understand your dreams with THE CREEI PROCESS.

---

[16] For a start, see the books by Allan Hobson in the References section.

"I don't care."

Another kind of resistance, ever growing in 21st-century America, is simple indifference. We are too busy with other pursuits of pleasure and entertainment to bother with dream workshops. A CREEI Workshop demonstrates vividly why a person should care simply by doing THE CREEI PROCESS and experiencing the results. The problem is getting them to the workshop.

"Dreams are so irrational that they cannot contribute to my decision-making."

Centuries of western thought have molded us into believing that rational linear thinking is the best way to make decisions and structure our lives. THE CREEI PROCESS values thinking and feeling equally. THE CREEI PROCESS itself is done by the waking self in a conscious act of granting a voice to the out-of-awareness self. It is a gesture of respect that the waking self rarely gives. The strange nature of dream content, where situations change rapidly and laws of physics seem regularly invalidated, are difficult to understand, but THE CREEI PROCESS brings these actions and behaviors into the rational realm. Still this attitude is strong in many people, even if they are not aware of it.

"Only wacko people are interested in dreams and other weird things."

This is another attitude that can be overcome by a rational approach to understanding meaning like THE CREEI PROCESS. A growing body of main-stream science continues to study the mysterious phenomenon of sleep and its dreams.[17] In addition, a growing body of evidence supports understanding out-of-body experiences (OBE), near-death experiences (NDE) and other kinds of non-ordinary states. A prominent neuroscientist, Eben Alexander, has provoked a firestorm of discussion in his 2012 book, Proof of Heaven: A Neurosurgeon's

---

[17] See the books by Allan Hobson in the References section.

Journey into the Afterlife.[18] Also, physicist/psychologist, Arnold Mindell, has published his experiences on how to communicate with people in coma.[19]

Group Dynamics and The CREEI Process

People are complex, and when you bring them together into groups the complexity just compounds. Dream work is hard and deeply personal. How and to what depth participants in a CREEI workshop learn is greatly influenced by how they interact with the group.

As you tally CREEI scores, you may gain immediate perspective from the majority of answers to a given CREEI question. For example, if everyone in the group scores their dream as (−) or (?) for interaction or for emotion, you know without sharing the dream contents that something may be wrong in the group. You will better understand where the group is most vulnerable. As a group learns THE CREEI PROCESS together, leaders and participants become better equipped to understand each other.

CREEI Spreadsheet Sorting

Using a computerized score sheet and sorting it in different ways is helpful to keep track of the CREEI patterns and following trends. **Spreadsheets 2a** and **2b** are examples of what happened during a Workshop and follow-up Seminar conducted by Eugene for an engineering group. Things were not going well and its owner realized that a root cause was hostile interactions among the employees. He wanted it straightened out quickly. The employees were given the choice: participate in a workshop or find another job. So, of course, they came, one or two kicking and grumbling.

---

[18] Alexander, Eben
[19] Mindell, Arnold

Spreadsheet 2a. Engineering Workshop-Seminar Results. This is how the spreadsheet looks like after it becomes a seminar.

Dreamer	DateDrmd	Title	C	R	E	E	I	//	C	P	S	//	E	A	B	B	Ch1	Ch2	Ptn	Notes
BB	05/22/1991	Misconception	+	+	?	+	+	//	+	?	?	//	?							
BB	06/11/1991	Sumptuary Tax	+	+	+	+	+	//	+	?	?	//	?							
BB	06/26/1991	Crystallize	+	+	+	+	-	//	+	+	+	//	+							
FCD	06/06/1991	The Traveler	+	-	+	-	-	//	+	-	+	//	+							
FCD	06/07/1991	Two Houses in Mexico	+	+	?	+	+	//	+	+	+	//	+	+	+	+	RSB	ENK		
FCD	06/21/1991	Church meeting	+	+	+	+	+	//	-	+	+	//	?	+	+	+			2	
PS	05/22/1991	Relief	+	+	-	-	+	//	?	-	-	//	?	+	?	-			3,4	
PS	06/03/1991	Stabbing a man	+	+	+	-	+	//	?	?	-	//	-	+	+	+			4	
PS	06/19/1991	a. House	+	+	+	+	+	//	-	-	-	//	-	+	+	+	GR	Grp	4	
PS	06/19/1991	b. Bedroom	+	+	+	+	+	//	-	-	-	//	?	+	+	+	BS	Fam	1	
PS	06/23/1991	Ice Cream	+	+	+	-	-	//	-	-	+	//	+	+	+	?			3,4	
RG	05/22/1991	Accident	+	+	-	+	+	//	?	-	-	//	+	+	?	+	FC		4	
RG	05/25/1991	Map	+	+	+	+	+	//	+	?	+	//	-	+	?	+				
RG	06/04/1991	Gang shooting	+	+	+	+	-	//	?	-	+	//	-	+	?	-	JG		4	
RG	06/15/1991	Chaos	-	-	+	?	+	//	?	+	+	//	+	+	?	+	GS		2	
RG	06/26/1991	Help	+	+	+	+	+	//	-	+	+	//	+	+	+	+	DS		1	
SLH	05/22/1991	Organization	?	+	+	+	-	//	-	-	-	//	+	+	+	+				
SLH	05/29/1991	Dead Girl Lives	+	+	?	+	+	//	+	+	+	//	+	+	+	?	NLM	ENK	2	
SLH	06/05/1991	Fancy Dinner	+	+	+	-	+	//	-	+	+	//	-	-	+	?	FH		4	
SLH	06/10/1991	Small steel van	+	+	+	+	+	//	-	+	+	//	+	+	+	+				
SLH	06/19/1991	Shopping	+	+	+	-	-	//	-	-	+	//	+	+	+	+				
WCR	05/16/1991	Caution	+	+	-	-	?	//	-	-	+	//	+	+	?	?				
WCR	05/29/1991	a. Traveling	+	-	+	+	+	//	+	+	+	//	+	?	?	?				
WCR	05/29/1991	b. Resting & wondering	+	+	+	-	+	//	-	-	+	//	+	?	?	?				
WCR	05/31/1991	a. Doctor's Examination	+	+	+	+	+	//	+	+	+	//	+	+	+	+				
WCR	05/31/1991	b. Sailing Ship	+	+	+	-	+	//	+	-	+	//	+	+	+	+				
WCR	06/11/1991	Locker Room	+	+	+	+	+	//	-	+	-	//	+	-	+	+	JS			

Employees and management met every week for six sessions. Eugene kept track in a computer spreadsheet of the dream scores. As the data accumulated, sorted by meeting dates of the seminar, the sorting results by dreamer and date brought out some interesting insights. Two individuals were especially interesting, Raul and Paula (see **Spreadsheet 2b**). Raul had been a gang member, a tough guy, but a good worker. He was the one who objected most to coming to the seminar. Raul's scores evolved from ANTICIPATORY-TRAUMATIC to TRANSFORMATIVE over the course of the seminar.

Spreadsheet 2b. Dreams of Raul and Paula as extracted from 2a. (This shows two dream patterns moving towards transformation over time.).

Dreamer	DateDrmd	Title	C	R	E	E	I	//	C	P	S	//	E	A	B	B	Ch1	Ch2	Ptn	Notes
Paula	05/22/1991	Relief	+	+	+	-	?	//	?	+	+	//	?	+	?	-			2	
Paula	06/03/1991	Stabbing a man	+	+	-	-	+	//	-	-	-	//	-	+	?	-			3,4	
Paula	06/19/1991	a. House	+	+	+	+	+	//	-	-	-	//	?	+	+	+			4	
Paula	06/19/1991	b. Bedroom	+	+	+	+	+	//	?	-	-	//	?	+	+	+	GR	Grp	4	
Paula	06/23/1991	Ice Cream	+	+	+	+	+	//	+	+	+	//	+	+	+	+	BS	Fam	1	
Raul	05/22/1991	Accident	+	+	+	-	-	//	-	-	+	//	-	+	-	?			3,4	
Raul	05/25/1991	Map	+	+	+	+	+	//	?	+	-	//	+	+	?	+	FC		4	
Raul	06/04/1991	Gang shooting	+	+	+	+	+	//	+	-	-	//	-	+	?	+	JG		4	
Raul	06/15/1991	Chaos	+	+	+	+	+	//	+	?	?	//	+	+	?	-	GS		2	
Raul	06/26/1991	Help	+	+	+	+	+	//	+	+	+	//	+	+	+	+	DS		1	

During THE CREEI PROCESS, Raul experienced such deep self-awareness that he had far fewer conflicts with others in the company. The spreadsheet revealed his own direction and trends that he had not been aware of. He was so excited that he insisted on writing to Eugene about his experience (see APPENDIX E).

The other example was Paula, a "superwoman" who could do everything: family, career, church, service. Everything, except when her life stalled. She also wanted to be a writer and came to the seminar with writer's block. She simply had become exhausted by the stress at home and all the rest of her responsibilities.

As with Raul, Paula's dreams first scored ANTICIPATORY-TRAUMATIC, including a dream about "stabbing a man." In the last session, however, she did not even want to report the "Ice Cream" dream scored in **Spreadsheet 2b** because she judged it to be too trivial and thus embarrassing. She did not think it meant anything. However, when she went through the CREEI questions she was amazed that it scored TRANSFORMATIVE!

Eugene asked what had been happening to her during the seminar period, not knowing any significant contents from her dreams. She had chosen not to share during the 6-week seminar period. However, in thinking about the question, she realized that her life had become more peaceful and that she was writing again. She had come to the seminars hoping that her dreams would tell her how to relieve her stress. Simply meeting together and sharing her dreams had had a TRANSFORMATIVE effect that she was not aware of until she saw the evolving pattern. Sharing the contents of all her dreams was not necessary. The action of working with her dreams subtly addressed her needs.

The company rapidly shifted to profitable productivity as workers in the group understood each other and worked in better harmony.

Chapter 5

PRACTICAL ASPECTS OF TEACHING
THE CREEI PROCESS

In this chapter we turn from the theoretical to the practical. Let us say that you have read this book to this point, have recorded and scored a number of dreams and that it is time for you to share your understanding of CREEI with others. How do you do it? In this section, we will discuss some of the practical aspects of first teaching THE CREEI PROCESS to a group in a CREEI workshop, and then continue teaching the following seminar.

THE CREEI PROCESS becomes even more powerful when used in a group setting over a period of time, especially if that group has a common goal. It is said that a person does not really know a subject until they have taught it. So even if you have no intentions of ever teaching CREEI don't skip this chapter. Pretend that you will so you can learn even better. If you do teach you will find that each workshop is wonderfully different and that you as teacher will learn new things every time you present.

Conducting the Dream Workshop

First, arrange a date, time and location for presenting THE CREEI PROCESS. Then advertise it in any way you feel appropriate. Sometimes the workshop is for a select group, such as a group of co-workers in a business. In that case, the "recruiting" is done for you. If it is more of an open community event, you can advertise in the local newspapers, put out fliers or do personal recruiting. However you do it, make clear the time expectation. Participants are expected to attend the entire workshop session. If this is not made clear at the beginning, the workshop will likely be compromised. Ask them to bring a dream and a one or two-word title to work with, but clarify the essential point that they will not be required to reveal any dream content.

Let's consider the question of whether to charge a fee for participation. You may not want to charge a fee, but you may need to in order to cover costs of refreshments, handouts, and meeting room rental. Specify clearly ahead of time what the charge will be. We hope that there would never be a person denied entrance to a CREEI Workshop because of lack of funds.

You may wish to ask people to register ahead of time so that you can have enough materials ready. Perhaps you may want to limit the attendance to a predetermined number. A group of six to ten is ideal, although larger groups will work, too. The first time you do this limit attendance so that you learn with a smaller group.

We have found that making a packet of papers with material like some of the figures in this book is especially helpful for a person to take home and study. Be prepared.

The day comes. Allow an absolute minimum of three hours, preferably four, to do the initial workshop. Beyond that time people become dumb in one place and numb in the other. Here is a sample schedule for a four-hour workshop:

SAMPLE SCHEDULE FOR A FOUR HOUR CREEI WORKSHOP

0845	Gathering for light snacks
0900	Opening, Welcome, and Introductions
0910	Expectations and Ground Rules
0915	Play or sing an opening song to set the mood
0920	Dream Work Principles and Assumptions
0940	The CREEI Questions
1030	Patterns

1045   Break with light snacks

1130   Dream Recall Techniques

1200   How to Work with Dreams — Unlocking the Creative Process

1230   CREEI and IDL — Deep Listening

1245   Questions and discussion of follow-up seminars

1300   Close and make plans for follow-up seminar

Introduce yourself and how you came to learn about THE CREEI PROCESS. It is extremely important to ask people to turn off or silence cell phones and to refrain from taking any calls during the workshop. Ask them to be fully present for this time. Then go around the room asking participants to introduce themselves, at least by first name, and briefly express why they came and their expectations for the workshop. Some may already be somewhat familiar with THE CREEI PROCESS; most will be entirely new. Some will express their opinion that dreams are meaningless while others may view them as visitations from God. Some will be there because they want to be, some only because they feel required to be. Accept without judgment any reason given, but try to sense where the resistance in a given individual may be. You as the workshop leader will be much better prepared to deal appropriately with each individual. You will also get a good feeling for who is likely to be excessively loquacious and in need of gentle handling, and who will be reticent and in need of gentle encouragement.

Briefly describe THE CREEI PROCESS and make it clear that this is a safe place. Set the ground rule strictly that anything discussed in the workshop is confidential and is not to be discussed outside the room or at a later time. This is absolutely crucial to the success of the group process. If later you find that confidences have been violated, it is important that you deal with it firmly and fairly, so that the group knows that it has been recognized and dealt with.

We feel strongly that the best way to learn THE CREEI PROCESS is to first experience it, and only then to explain it. That is the pattern of this book. So, draw a diagram on the board as you see in **Spreadsheet 3a**, similar to **Spreadsheet 1**, leaving as many spaces as people. Include yourself and include your own dream. It does not need to be precise and tidy, as demonstrated in this figure.

Workshop date: _____

DREAMER	DREAM DATE	TITLE	C	R	E	E	I	CP	S	E	A	B	B	PIN	CHAR I	CHAR II	NOTES

Spreadsheet 3a. Hand-drawn empty whiteboard for a seminar. Just copy it on a whiteboard by hand. It doesn't have to be neat to work.

Then, invite people to give you their name or initials, a one- to two-word title for the dream and the date of the dream. Was it last night, last week or three decades ago? If a person does not have a dream that they remember, then ask them to recall an event or experience, or perhaps the first experience they remember in their life. It is unusual for a person to opt out of THE CREEI PROCESS completely, but that, too, must be respected. It is our experience that once they see how the process is going, they become more willing to participate.

Next, go through each of the twelve CREEI questions one at a time. First, describe each question and how to score it. Then go around the room asking people to rate their own dream for that particular question. For example, describe what "clear" means, and then ask people to score their dream plus, minus or question mark, while you fill in the form on the board. It will quickly become apparent if the description has been understood or not by the questions people ask or the lack of questions. This process generates many valid questions, and through the years, the whole process has evolved to be more effective because of the questions of participants. You will learn from them. Another point is that participants will quickly learn that they don't need to deal with content to participate.

After the TWELVE QUESTIONS are described, ask for the initials of the two most important and recognizable characters in their dream (assuming that the dream contains such characters) and add them to the two far right columns designated for that purpose in the spreadsheet. Make clear that this is optional in a public setting, but that it can be personally important for the individual group member as time goes on.

Finally, explain the system for categorizing the dream score in terms of four typical patterns: TRANSFORMATIVE, MOTIVATIONAL, ANTICIPATORY and TRAUMATIC. Then you as the leader can look at each person's dream and assess its pattern. Participants will soon understand which pattern fits a dream, and that anyone can do this without knowing anything about the content of the dream. It is appropriate to comment about how meaningful a TRANSFORMATIVE or

MOTIVATIONAL dream can be. And you can express sympathy concerning ANTICIPATORY and/or TRAUMATIC dreams. By this time your white board should look like **Spreadsheet 3b.**

DREAMER	DREAM DATE	TITLE	C	R	E	E	I	C	P	S	E	A	B	B	PTN	CHAR I	CHAR II	NOTES
EMB	4-1965	DRAGON	+	-	-	+	+	-	+	+	+	?.	?.		3,4	RS		
LBR	8-18-'19	FALLING	+	+	+	+	+	+	+	+	+	+	+		2	DT		
FTP	8-18-'19	TRAIN WRECK	+	+	?.	?.	+	-	+	+	+	+	+		3	BA	PK	PANIC
SND	8-16-'19	BALL GAME	+	+	+	+	+	+	+	+	+	+	+		1	CN	GA	CONFIDENCE
LMT	8-17-19	SLUDGE	+	?.	?+	+	+	-	-	+	+	?	??		3,4			
KRJ	8-15-'19	HOMEWARD	+	+	?.	??	+	+	+	+	+	+	+		2			

Spreadsheet 3b. Hand-drawn seminar whiteboard filled In. This was not a real seminar and does not depict any real people or dreams. It does not violate confidentiality.

Usually by the end of this time, people need a break. This is hard work. Give a five- to ten-minute break for bathroom and refreshments, but not too long. Keep the momentum going.

After the break and depending on the time available, discuss with the group some of the basics about the reasons for respecting dreams and accepting THE CREEI PROCESS fundamentals presented in CHAPTER 5. Discussing this can take a long time or short time depending on the time available. This can be discussed in subsequent seminar sessions.

Next, if you think it is appropriate and participants feel comfortable to do so, you can invite the participants to share their dream contents. You may want to be the first to share the content of the dream you brought, or there may be a participant who is eager to begin THE CREEI PROCESS. Handle this carefully and gently. Set limits if a person is becoming long-winded and dominating the process. Also, be alert to the tendency of a participant to interpret or guide another dreamer. Remember, it is the dreamer's dream! Regardless, be very clear that no one in the room is required to reveal the actual contents of their dreams.

There have been occasions when participants have had immediate and dramatic insights. One example happened when Eugene conducted a 30-minute mini workshop for fifty-five people. From the back of the room came a loud "aha!" near the end of the session. Afterwards, he invited the woman to talk about her insight after the session. The group had done the three-stanza poem exercise. The first stanza had been a nightmare, which she wrestled with in the second stanza and then transformed it in the third. It turned out that she was about to be married in a day or so, but her dream that morning had been a warning. On doing THE CREEI PROCESS exercise, she realized that the marriage was not a good idea. When she decided at that moment to end her marriage plans, she came to peace.

Frequently by the end of a Dream Workshop, people have a deer-in-the-headlights look because they have been introduced to so many new concepts. For one thing, their waking self is often severely resisting this challenge to its supremacy.

Emphasize that it is important that participants engage further in THE CREEI PROCESS soon after the workshop, while the concepts are fresh. Encourage them to begin a dream journal immediately. Ask the group about their interest in follow-up dream seminars. If participants show interest, schedule it right away so that people have a time frame in which to begin to exercise their new skills. End the session with clear direction about what to do next.

Be sure to thank participants for coming and acknowledge the hard work that they have put in during the workshop. In your hand-out materials, you may want to provide participants with your contact information, as you deem appropriate. Invite people to contact you for clarification or guidance.

Conducting the Dream Seminar

The Dream Seminar is a regular follow-up to the Dream Workshop. We have found that THE CREEI PROCESS has optimal results in about six weekly 2-hour sessions, with an option to continue as desired. The nature of group dynamics and growth in a particular group dictates that participation in follow-up seminars be limited to workshop participants.

In the seminars, review the basics of scoring and rating dreams. It is inevitable that when people have gone home, they find they did not quite understand the scoring as well as they thought they had.

You may want to adopt the following ground rules for the follow-on seminar sessions.

- The seminar will meet weekly for two hours. Six weeks of sessions is typically optimal.

- Be on time. The door will be closed and locked at the stated opening time and no one is admitted after that. We have learned that late comers can disrupt the process.

- No outside interruptions once the process has started. No phones, texts, uninvited visitors, etc.

- Do not share or discuss a dream with the group unless you are comfortable in doing so.

- Each person must set their own limits. If a person becomes uncomfortable, they may stop active participation at any point, but ask them to please not get up and leave. This also disrupts the process.

- All dream material shared is confidential. It is crucial that people understand this and abide by it. The group process is severely threatened without a clear agreement on confidentiality. Keep emphasizing this.

- The group task is to listen to and help the dreamer.

- CREEI is nonjudgmental. It assumes that dreams are neither bad nor good. They just are, like feelings.

- CREEI assumes that all dreams have meaning. THE CREEI PROCESS assumes that dream fragments and nightmares rank equally important with dreams that are lucid personal visions and revelations.

- CREEI does not claim to be therapy. Rather, it is a simple method of self-evaluation. It is deliberately non-interpretive. It may, however, arouse in some the realization that they need professional help. This is to be encouraged.

- The dreamer, himself or herself, is the best interpreter and is the final authority of his/her own process.

Dream seminars usually go more quickly than the initial workshops. With each session the gray areas of understanding this process become fewer and fewer. Making space for exploring these gray areas brings deeper understanding of the material presented here as well as potential for an improved method.

Not all questions can be answered in this little book. The important thing is that the group must feel free to question and move ahead by understanding and supporting each other personally and collectively.

Begin each session with the blank spreadsheet as illustrated in **Spreadsheet 3a** Then score the dream of each participant. Typically, early in a given seminar you will see a lot of patterns in categories three and four. In a seminar where we go through our dreams and the group gets to know its members, it is not unusual to find that the patterns move toward MOTIVATIONAL and TRANSFORMATIVE. When you get to the TRANSFORMATIVE pattern, it usually contains wisdom and a useful message.

A dream is not only about one person. It can have implications for the whole group, and having the group aware of one person's dream can be a catalyst for understanding, maturation, and change for the whole group.

PART THREE

BROADER USES OF THE CREEI PROCESS

Chapter 6

Until now this book has looked at dreams provided by either the authors or their friends. When you begin to look you will find dreams reported in a wide variety of places.

Scientific Discoveries in Dreams

Sometimes we come to greater understandings during our sleep. Often when we are faced with a big decision, we want to "sleep on it." During sleep our out-of-awareness mind sorts out problems and helps us to understand them more clearly. In this way scientific discoveries are sometimes made in dreams.[20] Perhaps the most well-known example of scientific breakthrough from a dream had to do with the model of how benzene is structured and that it is actually a ring. Friedrich August Kekulé (1829–1896) was struggling with this issue when he dozed off on a bus. Here is his story:

> ### Friedrich August Kekulé
> BENZENE RING STRUCTURE, UNDATED
> *I was returning by the last bus, riding outside as usual, through the deserted streets of the city. ... I fell into a reverie, and lo, the atoms were gamboling before my eyes. Whenever, hitherto, these diminutive beings had appeared to me, they had always been in motion. Now, however, I saw how, frequently, two smaller atoms united to form a pair; how a larger one embraced the two smaller*

---

[20] https://www.theepochtimes.com/5-scientific-discoveries-made-in-dreams_1380669.html

ones; how still larger ones kept hold of three or
even four of the smaller, whilst the whole kept
whirling in a giddy dance. I saw how the larger
ones formed a chain, dragging the smaller ones
after them but only at the ends of the chains. ...The
cry of the conductor, "Clapham Road," awakened
me from my dreaming; but I spent a part of the
night in putting on paper at least sketches of these
dream forms.

CREEI SCORE: . . . . . **+++++//−++//++++**

MOTIVATIONAL

We know of several other examples. Dmitri Mendeleev (1834–1907) had a dream that showed him how the periodic table was formed. Niels Bohr [1885–1962] dreamed of the model for the atom being like planets revolving around the sun. Elias Howe (1819–1867) was inspired by a dream to understand how to perfect the sewing machine. Albert Einstein had a dream in which he was riding down a snow slope on a sled so fast that all of the colors blended together. This inspired him to consider how things might look if you were going the speed of light.[21] Something is happening during sleep in which our minds work on problems and present images of their solution. This ought not to be ignored.

Dreams in Literature

It is possible to gain a better understanding of a culture by looking at the dreams in its literature, whether those be fictional or sacred texts. In fiction, sometimes the dreams are real dreams of the author, which guide the creation of plot and story. Sometimes the author uses the dream as a tool for advancing the plot by revealing the inner workings of the character.

---

[21] Ibid.

Dreams in Sacred Scripture

CREEI can be used to track the dreams found in the Judeo-Christian scriptures. We leave open the possibility that dreams can be communications from outside of yourself, like from God. That is how most of the Bible dreams were interpreted by the dreamer. It is clear that most are either ANTICIPATORY or ANTICIPATORY-TRAUMATIC. That is not unusual in the Bible. These people often experienced incredible things that frightened them tremendously.

Dreamer	DateDrmd	Title	C	R	E	E	I	//	C	P	S	//	E	A	B	B	Ch1	Ch2	Ptn	Notes
Abram	Gen. 15:12	God's Covenant w Abram	+	-	+	+	?	//	?	+	-	//	?	+	+	+	Lord		3,4	First recorded dream in Bible
Abmlch	Gen. 20:3	Stay away from Abram's wife	+	+	+	+	?	//	+	+	-	//	+	+	?	+	God		2	God warns Abinelech
Jacob	Gen. 28:12	Jacob's Ladder	+	-	-	+	?	//	+	+	-	//	+	+	?	?	Lord		3	the naming of Beth-el
Laban	Gen. 31:24	God to Laban about Jacob	+	?	?	+	?	//	+	+	?	//	+	+	?	?	God	Jacob	3	
Josph	Gen. 37:5	a. Wheat sheaves bowing	+	+	+	-	?	//	+	+	+	//	+	+	?	?	bros		3	Joseph tells his dream to brothers
Josph	Gen. 37:5	b. Stars, etc. bowing	+	+	-	+	?	//	+	+	+	//	+	+	?	?			3	Joseph tells his dream to brothers
Butler	Gen. 40:8	Vine, grapes and Paraoh's cup	+	?	+	-	+	//	+	+	+	//	+	+	?	+	Phrh		3	Joseph interprets
Baker	Gen. 40:16	Bread for Pharoah	+	?	+	?	?	//	?	+	+	//	?	+	?	?	Phrh		3,4	Joseph interprets
Pharo	Gen. 41:1	Pharoah's 1st dream	+	?	?	?	?	//	?	?	?	//	?	?	?	?			3,4	Joseph interprets
Pharo	Gen. 41:5	Pharoah's 2nd dream	+	?	?	?	?	//	?	?	?	//	?	?	?	?			3,4	Joseph interprets
Man	Judg. 7:13	Gideon's Man's dream	+	?	?	?	?	//	+	+	+	//	+	+	?	?			3,4	Sword of Gideon
Solmn	1Kgs. 3:5	Solomon's dream	?	+	+	+	?	//	+	+	+	//	+	+	?	?	Lord		1	Negotiating for wisdom
Nebcnzr	Dan. 2:1	Nebuchadnezzar's 1st dream	?	?	?	?	?	//	+	+	?	//	+	?	?	?			3,4	
Nebcnzr	Dan. 2:19	Daniel's dream for Nebuchadnezzar	+	?	?	?	?	//	?	?	?	//	+	?	?	?	Son	Ancnt	3,4	Daniel dreams & interprets
Danl	Dan. 7:1	4 winds & 4 beasts	+	-	-	-	?	//	+	-	-	//	+	?	?	?			3,4	
Joseph	Matt. 1:20	Take Mary to wife	+	-	+	-	?	//	+	+	+	//	+	+	+	+	Angel		3	Birth of Jesus foretold
Joseph	Matt. 2:12	Flee to Egypt	+	-	-	-	?	//	+	+	+	//	+	+	+	+	Angel		3	Escaping Harod's plot
Joseph	Matt. 2:19	Return to Israel	+	?	-	-	?	//	+	+	?	//	+	+	+	+	Angel		3	After Harod's death
Pilot wife	Matt.27:19	Jesus is just	+	?	?	?	?	//	?	?	-	//	?	?	?	?			3,4	Confronting chief priests
Peter	Acts. 10:9-16	Sheet with animals	+	+	+	+	+	//	+	+	-	//	+	+	?	+	God		2	God commanding eating unclean meat

Spreadsheet 4. Biblical dreams. This represents a good survey of dreams from the Hebrew and Christian Bibles.

CHAPTER 6 DREAMS FROM OTHER SOURCES

Not scored in Spreadsheet 4 is an interesting passage from a lesser-known erotic book of the Bible, the Song of Solomon. In this passage, the woman dreams of her lover.

Lover from Song of Solomon
A TROUBLED LOVE

(SONG OF SOLOMON 5:2-8, NEW REVISED STANDARD VERSION).

I slept, but my heart was awake. Listen! My beloved is knocking. "Open to me, my sister, my love, my dove, my perfect one; for my head is wet with dew, my locks with the drops of the night." I had put off my garment; how could I put it on again? I had bathed my feet; how could I soil them? My beloved thrust his hand into the opening, and my inmost being yearned for him. I arose to open to my beloved and my hands dripped with myrrh, my fingers with liquid myrrh, upon the handles of the bold. I opened to my beloved, but my beloved had turned and was gone. My soul failed me when he spoke. I sought him, but did not find him; I called him, but he gave no answer. Making their rounds in the city, the sentinels found me; they beat me, they wounded me, they took away my mantle, those sentinels of the walls. I adjure you, O daughters of Jerusalem, if you find my beloved, tell him this: I am faint with love.

CREEI SCORE: . . . . . **++?++?//?--//?+??**

ANTICIPATORY-TRAUMATIC

The Q'ran also has many references to dreams, indicating the great importance attached to dreams by Islamic peoples. Out of respect for those sacred texts we will not quote them here, but encourage the interested reader to dive further into this subject.

Dreams in Fiction

A consistent literary device through much of literature is to use dreams as an author's way of describing the inner workings of their character's mind.[22] A number of popular works of literature have either had their origins in the dreams of their author or used the device of dreams to further the plot. These include The Strange Case of Dr. Jekyll and Mr. Hyde by Robert Louis Stevenson, Frankenstein by Mary Shelley, Stuart Little by E.B. White, Jane Eyre by Charlotte Bronte, Wuthering Heights by Emily Bronte and the poem "Kubla Kahn" by Samuel Taylor Coleridge. Jack Kerouac published his dreams in Book of Dreams.[23]

Profound insights into the meaning of these works of literature can be made by applying THE CREEI PROCESS to them.

Here are the opening paragraphs from Alice's Adventures in Wonderland by Lewis Carroll. Consistent with other dreams in this book we place the dream part in italics.

Alice

(fictional character in Alice in Wonderland)
ALICE DOWN THE RABBIT HOLE,[24] undated
Alice was beginning to get tired of sitting by her sister on the bank and having nothing to do.... So, she was considering, in her own mind (as well as she could, for the hot day made her feel sleepy and stupid), whether the pleasure of making a daisy-chain would be worth the trouble of getting up and

---

[22] https://www.dreams.co.uk/sleep-matters-club/10-unforgettable-dreams-in-literature-from-the-top-authors/ and https://www.bachelorsdegreeonline.com/blog/2010/15-famous-books-inspired-by-dreams/.
[23] Unfortunately, Kerouac's dreams are not dated, so it is impossible to track the writing career of this well-known Beat Generation writer chronologically.
[24] Carroll, Lewis 25-26.

picking daisies, when suddenly a White Rabbit
with pink eyes ran close by her.

  There was nothing so remarkable in that; nor
did Alice think it so much out of the way to hear the
Rabbit say to itself, "Oh dear! Oh Dear! I shall be
too late!" (When she thought it over afterwards it
occurred to her that she ought to have wondered at
this, but at the time it all seemed quite natural);
but, when the Rabbit actually took a watch out
of its waistcoat-pocket, and looked at it, and then
hurried on, Alice started to her feet, for it flashed
across her mind that she had never before seen a
rabbit with either a waistcoat-pocket, or a watch to
take out of it, and burning with curiosity, she ran
across the field after it, and was just in time to see
it pop down a large rabbit-hole under the hedge. In
another moment down went Alice after it, never
once considering how in the world she was to get
out again."

CREEI SCORE: . . . . . **+?++?//?++//++?+**

ANTICIPATORY

Virtually the entire rest of the book is a dream, and only ends
with Alice awakening from her sleep and relating to her sister all of her
adventures. From this first dream scene we learn that Alice is having a
great deal of problem responding to her situation, interacting with the
rabbit (though she certainly interacts with the rabbit-hole), and the
scene is not complete. In fact, the scenes rarely achieve good completion throughout the book. Because she is not interacting well with the
Rabbit she has no way of expressing her love for it. Viewing the scene
through the CREEI viewpoint we can relate the bizarre tale better to
our own lives.

Several dreams from Leo Tolstoy are in APPENDIX D.

Dreams of Historical Figures

It seems only appropriate to start this section looking at the dreams of the late 19th-century giants in the field of dreams, Sigmund Freud and Carl Jung.

SIGMUND FREUD

In his classic book, The Interpretation of Dreams, Freud included at least forty-seven of his own dreams. They are not dated, so they cannot be used to track the progression of his career in psychiatry, but it is nevertheless interesting to submit some to THE CREEI PROCESS. In listing Freud's dreams in **Spreadsheet 5**, notice that in the column titled "DateDrmd" we do not know the dates of his dreams. However, the numbers depict a sequence as they appear in Freud's classic, "The Interpretation of Dreams." Since dream 12 contains three scenes, we treat each scene as a separate dream. Thus, we score this dream as 12a, 12b and 12c in **Spreadsheet 5**. The remaining five dreams are in APPENDIX C.

Dreamer	DateDrmd	Title	C	R	E	E	I	//	C	P	S	//	E	A	B	B	Ch1	Ch2	Ptn	Notes
Sigmund Freud	9	Irma's Illness	+	+	+	+	+	//	-	?	+	//	+	+	+	-	Irma	Otto	4	Freud: "absurd"
Sigmund Freud	12a	Dissecting Pelvis	+	+	?	-	-	//	?	+	+	//	+	+	?	+	Louise		3	Freud: "absurd"
Sigmund Freud	12b	Cab Ride thru House	+	-	-	-	?	//	?	+	?	//	+	-	?	?			3	Freud: "absurd"
Sigmund Freud	12c	Bridging a Chasm	?	+	?	+	?	//	?	?	?	//	+	?	+	+			3,4	Freud: "absurd"
Sigmund Freud	13	Goethe attacks Herr M	-	+	?	-	+	//	+	-	+	//	+	+	?	-			3,4	Freud: "absurd"
Sigmund Freud	15	Crowd of People	?	?	+	-	-	//	+	+	?	//	?	?	?	?			3	Freud: "absurd"
Sigmund Freud	16	New of Son from Front	+	+	+	-	+	//	-	+	+	//	?	+	+	+			4	Freud: "absurd"
Sigmund Freud	17	Running upstairs undressed	+	-	+	?	-	//	?	-	+	//	?	+	?	+	P		3,4	Freud: "absurd"
Sigmund Freud	18	Riding on horse	+	+	+	-	+	//	-	+	+	//	?	+	+	+			3,4	Freud: "absurd"

Spreadsheet 5. Dreams of Sigmund Freud. Look at how much Freud could have learned about himself if he had subjected his dreams to The CREEI Process.

Freud insisted that he could interpret dreams and he carved new territory with that claim. But look how Freud behaved in his dreams and see what it tells about him without interpretation. The first dream that Sigmund Freud himself subjected to extensive interpretation was called "Irma's Illness." He explains in the preamble that Irma was a woman who was both a family friend and a patient. Irma was getting better under his care, but not completely well.

Sigmund Freud

IRMA'S ILLNESS,[25] JULY 24, 1895

A large hall—numerous guests, whom we were receiving. —Among them was Irma. I at once took her on one side, as though to answer her letter and to reproach her for not having accepted my "solution" yet. I said to her, "if you still get pains, it's really only your fault." She replied "If you only knew what pains I've got now in my throat and stomach and abdomen.... It's choking me." I was alarmed and looked at her. She looked pale and puffy. I thought that after all I must be missing some organic trouble. I took her to the window and looked down her throat, and she showed signs of recalcitrance, like women with artificial dentures. I thought that there was really no need for her to do that. She then opened her mouth properly and on the right side I found a big white patch; at another place, I saw extensive whitish-gray scabs upon some remarkable curly structures, which were evidently modeled on the turbinal bones of the nose. I at once called in Dr. M., and he repeated the examination and confirmed it.... Dr. M. looked quite different from usual; he was pale, he walked with a limp

---

[25] Ibid., 139-140. Freud did not title his dreams, so these are our titles in this section for dreams and scenes.

and his chin was clean shaven.... My friend Otto
was now standing beside her as well, and my friend
Leopold was perusing her through her bodice and
saying," She has a dull area low down on the left."
He also indicated that a portion of the skin on the
left shoulder was infiltrated. (I noticed this, just as
he did, in spite of her dress.) ... M. said, "There's
no doubt it's an infection, but no matter; dysentery
will supervene and the toxin will be eliminated."
... We were directly aware, too, of the origin of her
infection. Not long before, when she was feeling
unwell, my friend Otto had given her an injection
of a preparation of propyl, propyls...propionic
acid.... trimethylamine (and I saw before me the
formula printed in heavy type). ... Injections of that
sort ought not to be made so thoughtlessly. ... And
probably the syringe had not been clean.

CREEI SCORE: . . . . . **+??++//−?+//++−−**
ANTICIPATORY-TRAUMATIC

This was followed by nearly nine pages of explanation and inter-pretation. In the end, he wrote, "When the work of interpretation has been completed, we perceive that a dream is the fulfillment of a wish."[26] In this dream Freud's wish was to be free of responsibility for Irma's illness and the content of the dream was a fulfillment of that wish.[27]

Below are two of the seven dreams taken from Freud's classic, "The Interpretation of Dreams." The second dream in **Spreadsheet 5** ("12") has three scenes, all of which are CREEI scored separately. The remaining five dreams are in APPENDIX C.

---

[26] Ibid., 154
[27] Ibid., 151

Freud was well aware of his dreams but frequently dismissed them when he labeled them as absurd. We think that if he had had THE CREEI PROCESS available to him he would have seen more clearly the importance of those dreams, as they virtually always score as ANTICIPATORY or TRAUMATIC or both.

This next dream has three scenes.

Sigmund Freud

DISSECTING MY OWN PELVIS,[28] UNDATED

Scene 1. Dissecting my Own Pelvis - Old Bruecke must have set me some task; STRANGELY ENOUGH, it related to a dissection of the lower part of my own body, my pelvis and legs, which I saw before me as though in the dissecting-room, but without noticing their absence in myself and also without a trace of any gruesome feeling. Louise N was standing beside me and doing the work with me. The pelvis had been eviscerated, and it was visible now in its superior, now in its inferior, aspect, the two being mixed together. Thick flesh-coloured protuberances (which, in the dream itself, made me think of hemorrhoids) could be seen. Something which lay over it and was like crumpled silver-paper had also to be carefully fished out.

CREEI SCORE: . . . . . **++?-+//-?+//++?+**

ANTICIPATORY-TRAUMATIC

Scene 2. Cab Ride through House - I was then once more in possession of my legs and was making my way through the town. But (being tired) I took a cab. To my astonishment, the cab drove in through the door of a house, which opened and allowed it

---

[28] Ibid., 489-90. The names of the dreams Freud presented and the division into scenes and their names are ours.

to pass along a passage which turned a corner at its end and finally led into the open air again.

CREEI SCORE: . . . . . **+---+//?++//++-?**

Scene 3. Bridging a Chasm - Finally I was making a journey through a changing landscape with an Alpine guide who was carrying my belongings. Part of the way he carried me too, out of consideration for my tired legs. The ground was boggy; we went 'round the edge; people were sitting on the ground like Red Indians or gipsies [sic] among them a girl. Before this I had been making my own way forward over the slippery ground with a constant feeling of surprise that I was able to do it so well after the dissection. At last we reached a small wooden house at the end of which was an open window. There the guide set me down and laid two wooden boards, which were standing ready, upon the window-sill, so as to bridge the chasm which had to be crossed over from the window. At this point I really became frightened about my legs, but instead of the expected crossing, I saw two grown-up men lying on wooden benches that were along the walls of the hut, and what seemed to be two children sleeping beside them. It was as though what was going to make the crossing possible was not the boards but the children. I awoke in a mental fright.

CREEI SCORE: . . . . . **+??+?//???//++?+**

ANTICIPATORY-TRAUMATIC

Freud judged this 3-scened dream as absurd, but since we feel that it is wrong to judge a dream, we believe that Freud overlooked important information about his own life that this dream was trying to say to him. Nevertheless, we will not interpret that for him.

The remaining five dreams can be found in APPENDIX C, all of which Freud interpreted as "absurd."

In his book *Myths to Live By*, Joseph Campbell wrote: "Freud... judged the worlds of myth, magic, and religion negatively, as errors to be refuted, surpassed, and supplanted finally by science.... An altogether different approach is represented by Carl G. Jung, in whose view the imageries of mythology and religion serve positive, life-furthering ends."

CARL G. JUNG

Jung did not publish as many dreams as Freud. In the following dream he reported a time when he was treating a young woman in her twenties who had evolved to a lifestyle where she dressed provocatively and was sexually promiscuous.

Carl Jung
WOMAN ON A TOWER,[29] UNDATED

I was walking down a highway through a valley in late afternoon sunlight. To my right was a steep hill. At its top stood a castle, and on the highest tower there was a woman sitting on a kind of balustrade. In order to see her properly, I had to bend my head far back. I awoke with a crick in the back of my neck. Even in the dream I had recognized the woman as my patient.

CREEI SCORE: . . . . . **+??+−//−++//++−+**

ANTICIPATORY

---

[29] Jung, G.C. Memories, Dreams, Reflections, 133.

Jung realized that he had been looking down on this woman and judging her. His dream helped him to change his attitude and become less judgmental of her lifestyle.

Jung could have used CREEI terminology to describe his dream without disclosing the dream narrative (these are our interpretations), "I had a clear dream in which my role was not well-defined and so I was not responding rigorously. I had strong emotions, but was not expressing myself well, nor was I interacting with other dream characters. The dream came to an abrupt end with a startling revelation to me about how I judge other people by their appearances. It was a pleasant dream mostly, I was secure and I had good self-esteem. I was being authentic, but because I was not interacting, I could not say that the other person in my dream was experiencing their own beauty. I did, though, feel that I moved to a higher level of self when I realized how judgmental I can be." Doing this kind of narrative may not have the same imaginative impact on the listener/reader, but it goes into greater detail about how Jung was behaving in the dream. By using terms more comparable to how he behaves in his waking life he might have understood himself better than when he was immersed in the strangeness of the dream imagery.

HELEN SCHUCMAN

Helen Schucman authored A Course in Miracles (ACIM), but refused to have her name associated with the book during her lifetime.[30] She was a psychiatrist, a Jewish atheist, and having struggles with her colleagues. She realized that there must have been something better, so she began to work with one of her colleagues, who was her boss. During the summer of 1965, she began to be aware of her dreams, which were posthumously published by some of her friends.[31]

---

[30] Schucman, Helen.
[31] Skutch, Robert.

Look what happened in her dreams as she was being prepared in some mysterious way because she was sincere about a resolution to the struggles with her colleagues. Notice how the patterns move toward TRANSFORMATIVE. The person who identifies himself in the dream is Jesus and that was huge for her. This is a good example of how the patterns change as we track her dreams and compared the patterns' evolution to TRANSFORMATIVE. She had no idea that ACIM was coming.

Dreamer	DateDrmd	Title	C	R	E	E	I	//	C	P	S	//	E	A	B	B	Ch1	Ch2	Ptn	Notes
H Schucman	06/01/1965	1a Kneeling chained bowed priestess (P)	+	-	-	-	-	//	?	?	?	//	?	?	?	?	P		3,4	nearby fire rises hi abv P's head
H Schucman		1b P raises head, chains begin to fall away	+	+	-	-	-	//	?	?	-	//	?	?	?	?	P	WT	3,4	
H Schucman		1c P stands up, chain remnand on left wrist	+	+	+	+	-	//	?	?	?	//	?	?	?	?	P		3,4	Fire blaes brighter as P stands
H Schucman		1d P looks at me, but I look away	+	+	+	+	-	//	+	+	+	//	+	+	+	+	P		3,4	
H Schucman		1e Finally I look at P and weep	+	+	+	+	+	//	+	+	+	//	+	+	+	+	P		1	
H Schucman		2a In tethered gondola rowing nowhere	+	-	-	-	-	//	?	?	?	//	?	?	?	?	WT		3	Sequined gondolier stands near watching
H Schucman		2b Bull fighter Bill in spectacular constume	?	+	?	?	?	//	+	?	?	//	?	?	?	?	WT		3,4	Bill as Bullfighter
H Schucman		2c Witch doctor Bill in feathers and jewels	+	+	+	+	+	//	+	+	+	//	+	+	?	?	WT		3,4	
H Schucman		3a Am high priestess in Egyptian temple	+	+	+	+	-	//	+	+	+	//	+	+	-	-	WT		3,4	Blazing light on altar from above
H Schucman		3b Ready to kill Bill	+	+	+	+	?	//	+	+	-	//	+	+	-	-	WT		4	
H Schucman		3c Outside temple facing desert	+	+	+	+	-	//	+	+	+	//	+	+	?	-	WT		3,4	
H Schucman		4a In monastary	+	+	+	+	+	//	+	+	+	//	+	+	?	-	WT		4	Bill as Franciscan monk in Spain
H Schucman		4b P cloistered in small white marble temple	?	+	-	?		//	+	+	+	//	+	+	+	+	WT		3	plain altar w flame & white smoke, people
H Schucman		4c P praying & healing others	+	+	+	+	+	//	+	+	+	//	+	-	+	+	WT		1	
H Schucman		5a Black slaves in America	+	+	+	+	+	//	+	?	+	//	?	+	-	-	WT		4	
H Schucman		5b Am innocent priestess, praying at altar	+	+	+	+	?	//	+	+	+	//	+	+	+	+	WT		3,2	Small flame on plain wooden altar, Elohim
H Schucman		5c The altar within	+	+	+	+	+	//	+	+	+	//	+	+	+	+	WT	JC	1	Jesus kneels at altar w Bill & me, Voice
H Schucman		6a Abandoned boat, anchor in mud	+	+	+	+	-	//	+	+	+	//	+	+	+	+	JC?		3	
H Schucman		6b Man helps free boat & begin journey	+	+	+	+	+	//	+	+	+	//	+	+	+	+	JC?		1	
H Schucman		6c Man helps steer boat in choppy water	+	+	+	+	+	//	+	+	+	//	+	+	+	+	JC?		1	
H Schucman	10/20/1965	6d Man, peaceful water, gold chain symbol	+	+	+	+	+	//	+	+	+	//	+	+	+	+	JC?		1	Symbol of miracle of reversal

Spreadsheet 6. Dreams of Helen Schucman. Her dreams evolved toward transformative with time.

WILFORD WOODRUFF

In the late 1800s, Wilford Woodruff became the fourth president of the Mormon Church.[32] In his autobiography,[33] he revealed a number of different dreams from different phases of his long life. **Spreadsheet 7** shows the list, with their CREEI scores.

---

[32] In August 2019, the church officially adopted its formal, legal name "The Church of Jesus Christ of Latter-day Saints" and stopped referring to itself as Mormon.
[33] Staker, Susan.

Spreadsheet 7. Dreams of Wilford Woodruff over his lifetime.

Dreamer	DateDrmd	Title	C	R	E	E	I	//	C	P	S	//	E	A	B	B	Ch1	Ch2	Ptn	Notes
W Woodruff	02/19/1840	Cannibal killing men & children	+	-	+	+	-	//	-	-	+	//	+	?	?	-			3,4	Struggles w hostile Methodist preachers
W Woodruff	02/26/1840	a. Catching many fish plus big one	+	+	+	+	-	//	-	+	+	//	+	+	+	?			2	aftr preaching & baptising preacher
W Woodruff	02/26/1840	b. Catching super big fish	+	+	+	+	?	//	-	+	+	//	+	+	+	?			2	aftr preaching & baptising preacher
W Woodruff	06/08/1840	Church on fire	+	+	?	?	-	//	?	+	+	//	+	?	?	?			3,4	
W Woodruff	10/25/1840	Catching and eating fish	+	+	+	+	+	//	+	+	+	//	+	+	+	+	PWC		1	aftr successful preaching
W Woodruff	01/04/1841	Wife and child	+	-	+	+	-	//	+	-	+	//	+	+	?	?	PWC		3	aftr prayer for success
W Woodruff	01/06/1841	a. Serpents and dragons	+	-	+	+	-	//	?	+	+	//	?	+	+	-			3,4	Trouble preaching in London
W Woodruff	01/06/1841	b. Tasting large fruit	+	+	+	+	+	//	?	?	+	//	+	+	+	?			2	Trouble preaching in London
W Woodruff	01/07/1841	Wild pears turn into hanging sheep	+	+	+	+	+	//	?	+	+	//	+	+	+	?			1	letter frm wife asking him to come home
W Woodruff	01/15/1841	Catching many large fish w hands	+	+	+	+	+	//	+	+	+	//	+	+	+	+			1	after baptising success in London
W Woodruff	12/01/1841	"Disagreeable dream"	?	?	?	?	?	//	?	?	+	//	?	?	?	?	JSJr		3,4	dream judged from Devil and disregarded
JSJr	02/03/1844	a. Steam boat sinks w all on board	+	+	+	+	+	//	+	+	+	//	+	+	+	?			2	
JSJr	02/03/1844	b. Boasting	+	+	+	+	+	//	+	+	+	//	+	+	+	?			2	
JSJr	02/03/1844	c. Swimming in rough waters	+	+	+	+	+	//	+	+	+	//	+	+	+	?			1	
W Woodruff	01/19/1847	About to give birth	+	+	+	?	+	//	+	-	+	//	+	+	+	+	BrS		2	aftr orgnizg fmly co. & being sustained
W Woodruff	05/13/1847	Seeing temple at journey's end	+	+	+	+	+	//	+	+	+	//	+	+	+	+			1	traveling west w the Twelve
W Woodruff	03/05/1848	Meeting Joseph & Hyrum in Heaven	+	?	?	?	+	//	?	+	+	//	?	+	?	?	JSJr	HS	3	after day in ofc on BY's history
W Woodruff	11/17/1857	Impending Indian war	?	+	-	+	+	//	+	+	+	//	+	+	?	?	JMB		3	aftr day reading pers histories
W Woodruff	11/18/1857	Enemy attack	+	-	+	+	+	//	?	+	+	//	?	+	?	?			3,4	
W Woodruff	03/30/1859	a. Battle w rattle snake	+	-	+	+	+	//	-	+	+	//	+	+	+	+			3,2	
W Woodruff	03/30/1859	b. Ground covered w ripe apples	+	+	?	+	?	//	?	+	+	//	?	?	?	+	PAW	LS	3	fulfillment of earlier dream
PCW	04/04/1859	marriage of daughter	+	?	?	+	?	//	?	+	+	//	?	?	?	+	CL	JSJr	3	WW wife's dream abt death of boy
PCW	01/31/1861	Little Charles with Joseph	+	-	+	+	+	//	+	+	+	//	+	+	+	+			3	
W Woodruff	09/04/1873	a. US flag tattered; N to S in sky	+	-	+	+	-	//	-	+	+	//	+	+	?	?			3	
W Woodruff	09/04/1873	b. Constitution tied tgther w ropes	+	-	+	+	-	//	-	-	+	//	+	+	?	?	USG		3	
W Woodruff	09/04/1873	c. Eagle carrying Pres. Grant off	+	-	+	+	-	//	?	+	+	//	+	+	?	?	JVG	McM	1	
W Woodruff	09/07/1873	a. Talking to JMG and Sis McM	+	+	+	+	+	//	+	+	+	//	+	+	+	?			1	
W Woodruff	09/07/1873	b. Seeing dead arise	+	+	+	+	+	//	+	+	+	//	+	+	+	?	BpH		2	
W Woodruff	02/12/1879	In SLC counseld by Bp Hunter	+	-	+	+	+	//	+	-	+	//	+	+	+	?	JWT	12	2	on the underground
W Woodruff	12/16/1879	Pres Tylr seal'g all plural marg's	+	+	+	+	+	//	+	+	+	//	+	+	+	?	QV		1	WW judges and dismisses
W Woodruff	06/14/1880	Sealed to Queen Victoria	+	?	+	+	?	//	+	+	+	//	+	+	?	?			3	
W Woodruff	06/01/1882	Messenger abt spirits in prison	+	?	?	?	+	//	?	+	+	//	?	?	?	?			3	
W Woodruff	12/26/1882	Pres Young's counsel	+	-	+	+	-	//	+	-	+	//	+	+	?	?	BY	12	1	BY says WW "one born out of due time"
W Woodruff	03/06/1885	Blessed & ordained by BY w 12	+	+	+	+	+	//	+	+	+	//	+	+	+	?	BY	12	3	
W Woodruff	03/19/1894	Ben Franklin asks more work	+	+	+	+	+	//	+	+	+	//	+	+	+	?	BF		1	"Second anointing"
W Woodruff	05/17/1897	"Distressing dreams"	+	?	+	?	?	//	?	+	?	//	?	?	?	?			3,4	

When you look at his dreams you can see that the patterns are all over the map, but if you look right toward the end, you can see what happened just before the end of his life. His dreams became distressing. He would often have dreams in his early life when he was a missionary and after preaching, he often dreamed of catching fish. He was an ardent fisherman, but notice every time he was catching good fish, it was after successful preaching. As an old man in his nineties, he was not doing well. He had some powerful TRANSFORMATIVE dreams, but he was also having troubling dreams, ANTICIPATORY and TRAUMATIC.

With this collection of dreams, it is apparent that he may not really have understand his personal situation. He rose to become President and Prophet of the LDS Church and was looked to be the wisest and most inspired man of the Church. Yet he apparently did not understand many of his dreams. Had he had access to THE CREEI PROCESS, he could have seen the evolution and changes he had experienced during his lifetime and perhaps been able to redirect his personal and church life better, especially at the end.

Chapter 7

OTHER APPLICATIONS FOR
THE CREEI PROCESS

S o far, discussing THE CREEI PROCESS has been exclusively in the context of seeking the meaning of your own dreams. However, as we stated much earlier in the book, CREEI has much broader applications.

CREEI and Personal Life Events

Though more often applied to dreams, the CREEI questions can be applied to any personal life event. You can use these questions for self assessment as you look back on a situation and ask if you clearly understood it. Were you responding or just reacting; were your emotions high enough and were you expressing them; were you interacting with others and was the experience complete, pleasant, safe? Was your self-esteem high, were you being authentic; did your behavior enhance the lives of those around you, and were you growing in the experience? In the same way when another person is struggling you can ask these questions, and it is often that as a person answers them, he or she comes to greater understanding of their event. Thinking in terms of the CREEI questions allows you to understand better those around you as well as your group's dynamics.

THE CREEI PROCESS can be creatively applied to many other personal situations, such as experiences of artistic performances or exhibitions, or readings of poetry or prose, or beholding a sculpture, building, or landscape. You may even want to figure out how to apply it as you review in your mind an argument with a bully or a gentle encounter with a loved one.

While each situation is different, the questions help to compare that unique circumstance to a more universal set of standards that are your core values. A CREEI scan might go like this: I think that I will have a better life if I am mindful so that I clearly understand; I respond to situations rather than react; I express myself to myself and others; I perceive my true emotional response or lack of it; I interact with my environment and people; I have a feeling of completion because I have not procrastinated; I create a pleasant and safe situation; and I know that I am better for having learned from it, that I have been authentic in interacting with my surroundings, that the world is a better place for my having been here, and that I am moving to a more integrated level. By going through the TWELVE QUESTIONS it is possible to truly discover core values. And it may be that your review causes you to question whether you really live by your core values.

One way Bob has used the CREEI scan is to assess a day, either prospectively or retrospectively. This might include resolutions about the coming day or assessment as to how he did. He applies the methods for working with dreams to assess how he could transform the day to a transformational one. He writes:

"To make this day a transformational day I need to: remain mindful as much as I can, including how I dress and eat, so I need to make mindfulness a habit and experience of events clear; be responsive instead of merely reacting by knowing that there are going to be several situations today where this will be important so be alert for my possibilities; keep good emotions and reject the influence of others who might reduce the goodness of them; share my positive strong emotions with others by encouraging them; keep checking for loose ends to the situation and how I might plan to tie them up on the spot or in the future; look for pleasant situations and avoid the unpleasant; be alert to dangers, physical, mental, and emotional, and avoid them or defuse them; act in ways that build myself up in my own self-esteem; be authentic in what I do; always look for ways of how I might help others in any way that they need; and do activities that will help me to grow to fuller life."

THE CREEI PROCESS can be used by people with security clearances to share the meaning of their dreams without revealing the contents of the dreams, since classified information could possibly be revealed by sharing the story of the dream.

In a non-dream application of THE CREEI PROCESS it can possibly be applied by personnel managers for screening prospective employees. This was suggested by a personnel manager in an aerospace engineering company. He envisioned asking himself the TWELVE QUESTIONS in terms of how the applicant comes across to him in an employment interview so that he could better evaluate his opinion of the applicant.

Dreams may unlock creativity, whether through visual arts, music, or dance. A good example came following an early CREEI workshop. A professor of English with a specialty in creative writing at a large Western university attended the workshop as a skeptic. However, after she saw THE CREEI PROCESS in action, she became enthusiastic and used CREEI with her classes to help students in their creative writing.

You may want to use THE CREEI PROCESS to discuss your dream or behavior with a professional counselor or clergy person. If so, it will be more useful if they also are familiar with the process. They cannot interpret your dreams for you, but if they are familiar with THE CREEI PROCESS they can help you think about the dream more clearly. When you begin to present the dream to them in terms of CREEI scoring, most will be able to work with it better, even if they are not familiar with CREEI questions. If you relate that your self-esteem in the dream is low or the dream is unpleasant or you are passive in the dream, they will be better acquainted with your inner self and better able to help.

Knowing Another Person More Deeply

CREEI is a great way to get to know another person. "Tell me about your dreams" is a quick door opener, especially when you start asking the CREEI questions without asking for the content of the dream. As you run the dream through THE CREEI PROCESS you may be surprised at how quickly you get to know someone.

This applies even in situations when your initial impulse is to dislike someone. Abraham Lincoln has been quoted as saying, "I don't like that man. I must get to know him better."[34] Applying CREEI questions will get you through that first negative impression. CREEI bypasses the ego protection that most of us have built in. A deep friendship can be established quickly, especially when it comes from an attitude of trust and confidence. Usually, once that trust has been established, the other person will gladly share the contents of the dream as well. But that is not necessary.

Eugene commented, "I remember people by the dreams they share with me more than any other way, because I believe it anchors their truth for me more accurately than their appearance or behavior." A good example was when he first met the superintendent of our school system.[35] Gene Schmidt shared three dreams with Eugene at three different times in his tenure in our town: one at the beginning, one in the middle, and one toward the end. These dreams described the arc of his job. It is with his permission that we share these remarkable dreams with you.

Gene Schmidt
TIBETAN MONASTERY, 2008

Background: My sister was diagnosed with cancer that migrated ever deeper into her brain. The gift of surgery allowed her another year of life. During that time, I placed a hold on my plans to complete a PhD program. Instead, my wife and I took time to visit my sister when we could. Rather than worry about herself, my sister focused our time together on me and made me promise to finish my degree. She died before knowing I had finished my

---

[34] https://www.goodreads.com/quotes/5989-i-don-t-like-that-man-i-must-get-to-know.
[35] Los Alamos Public Schools.

degree work and graduated in 2008. Shortly after graduation, I had this dream. Dying of cancer is a terrible thing, yet my sister faced this terrible disease with dignity.

It was already midmorning as I rounded the corner on my steep climb up the narrow, hard-packed dirt path that trailed upward along a spiny mountainside ridge in Nepal. I noted with curiosity the absence of snow or ice along the trail. Looking farther up the mountainside, I caught my first glimpse of a polished log-framed Tibetan monastery with its iconic swept-wing rooflines. I paused for a moment to marvel at the site of the monastery, acknowledging to myself I still had a long, hard climb ahead. I really wasn't sure why I was making this climb, but somehow I knew making this climb had significance to me.

Just that quickly, my climb was finished. I stood before the monastery's wooden front porch. The noon sun was shining brightly above me as I swung a heavy wooden mallet against the large bronze bell. Responding to the sound of the bell, a rather small, well-rounded, bald, shirtless Buddhist monk greeted me with a smile. I followed him through hand-polished wooden double doors into a darkened chamber. It took a moment to adjust to the dimness of light inside.

The room was filled with a smoky blue cloud of incense. I paused before a large wooden prayer wheel. As I spun the wheel, the inner chamber lightened to reveal a large room constructed entirely of polished wood. I stood on a slightly elevated room encircled by a polished wooden railing. Many vertical support logs in the room were carved *with figures and runes whose symbols I did not understand. Near the center of the room, I noticed several similarly shirtless, chubby, bald, smiling monks, whose only clothing was a white woolen waist cloth extending toga style to their feet. All five monks were attending to a female, sitting on a stool in the middle of the chamber. Her bare back was turned to me.*

When the women turned her head to see me, I recognized the face of my sister who had recently died from brain cancer. She smiled and spoke soothingly. "I want you to know I am fine. I am no longer in pain. Tell them everything is going to be okay."

My attention shifted to a monk who was holding a round bronze dish. He smiled as white, almost-translucent steam began to emanate skyward from the dish. As the quantity of steam from the dish intensified, my sister slowly dissolved into the steam, leaving nothing except a sensation of genuine happiness in the chamber.

As I stood alone on the monastery porch, looking at valley below, I sensed the walk down would not be nearly as long as the trek up. My sister was in a better place, and so was I.

CREEI SCORE: . . . . . **+++?+//+++//++++**

MOTIVATIONAL

This dream became TRANSFORMATIVE as Gene Schmidt expressed the dream. The act of sharing the MOTIVATIONAL dream, of expressing it, shifted it to TRANSFORMATIVE, comforting, and confirming. Gene shared this dream with Eugene shortly after Gene's sister's death. In telling the dream, Gene Schmidt discovered how comforted he was by it because it described her in a mysterious place, a resolving place.

It also brought his grief process into a comforting and encouraging place. Eugene felt that he was able to have a deeper connection with this man quickly.

Gene Schmidt

SMALL BOAT DISTRESS, ABOUT 2012

Background: As work-related concerns with my supervisors mounted, I found myself facing the real possibility of resigning from my position as school superintendent. I loved my work and the community in which I worked. My decision was difficult but one I made nevertheless. In a wonderful moment of unexpected paradox, I was invited to stay for another year while the school board conducted a search for my replacement. It was shortly after my hiring for this extra year that I had this dream. Interestingly, the dream gave me strength that whatever happened next in life, I was ready to share my gifts.

Unlike other dreams that seemed tied to a serious event in my life, this dream occurred more out of curiosity for the way the world seemed to evolve around me. Dreams are like that. They sometimes are meant as a way to make sense of things—more of an opportunity for your mind to explore and wander with you along for the ride. This ride was interesting because in the busyness of peoples' lives, we forget to care about others.

The multistory glass-window building was enormous in both size and for the amount of work taking place inside. Despite being built right next to the ocean, hundreds of workers took no time to enjoy the beauty of the seascape just outside their windows. No one, it seemed, paid any attention

*to the waves as they lapped against the near shore
or the sailboat as it neared the dock next to the
building. Instead these many, many employees were
consumed with their work as they hammered away
at the computer keyboards. It was important work.
Everyone was busy, and I was their boss.*

*I was standing in the center of this maelstrom
of activity when I noticed that the weather outside
our glass enclosure was whipping the sea into a
frenzy. Then my attention focused on the sailboat
as the captain tried to tie it to the dock. As the waves
strengthened, it became apparent that the sailboat
was clearly in distress. I watched as the boat's owner
desperately tried to lash the boat more tightly to
its moorings. Despite his efforts, waves of seawater
pummeled the boat and smashed it against the
dock. The sailboat began to list and turn on its side.
The boat's captain was now clinging to the side of
his vessel.*

*The sailor looked imploringly at the
windowed building full of people working busily at
their stations. I looked first at the captain, who was
definitely going down with his ship, and then back
to my many employees, who, without any sense of
compassion or concern, continued their work.*

*I looked again at the captain and understood
his desperation. As our eyes met, I dashed from
the building and rushed to aid the sinking sailor.
I pulled the water-soaked captain to safety on the
dock. I then lashed the bow of the boat to a piling in
time to save the ship from entirely sinking.*

*The dream ended as I turned back toward my
office building. Staff watched through the window,
but no one had come to help. I found myself*

wondering, *"Why didn't anyone help? Why didn't anyone care?"*

CREEI SCORE: . . . . . **+++?+//+?+//++++**

Gene Schmidt was able to see the big picture, inside and outside of his work situation. No one inside was aware of the external situation, and he had to react and respond. Eugene correctly assessed that Gene Schmidt was a man of action, compassion, and vision.

Gene Schmidt
I AM HERE TO HELP YOU FIX
YOUR PROBLEMS, 2014?

The day was warm, and by the height of the sun, I could tell it was approaching noon. The sky was blue, and there was no hint of rain. The old white 1960-ish Ford two-ton dump truck that my brother was diving crawled slowly up the steep, narrow, potholed road. My brother somehow managed to keep the dump truck from careening off the mesa's roadside.

Through the truck's open passenger-side window, I looked down with alarm as the truck's rear duals spit rocks over the cliff as the truck chewed its way toward the mesa top high above us. With each rock chuck, the truck churned and bounced closer to the top. My big brother, Bill, who was driving, smiled reassuringly and said, "I am here to help you fix your problem."

My problem was to fill the many potholes that littered the mesa top. And with that, Bill guided the much-dented and well-rusted dump truck to the crest of the mesa for the first of what would be many trips. Looming before us were countless numbers of potholes. I knew then that I needed the help.

And help he did. I thought that this is what big brothers are supposed to do. My big brother, who had died many years before my dream, had driven trucks all his life. Now he was here to help me when I needed it most. It did not matter to him that the journey was extremely dangerous or that the holes were many. He smiled confidently though the many ascents and descents of the mesa brought us face-to-face with driving peril. Down, up, and down again for the rest of the day—each truckload filling three holes, each trip a desperate climb, each trip a challenge to the laws of gravity and a physical challenge to the driver's skill, each trip one more call for the truck to crawl its way back up the steep, narrow, rock-filled, pothole-scarred road. One dump truckload of dirt at a time until the entire mesa top was leveled and the work was done.

As we filled the last hole, my brother and the dump truck dissolved and were gone. Just as quickly, I was walking down a newly paved highway, which paralleled a railroad track. I was savoring the tasty taco from a well-filled plate of Mexican food that I was eating as I walked the highway.

Off in the distance, I noticed a new red pickup that appeared to be stalled in the middle of the railroad crossing. The hood of the truck was up, which confirmed my suspicion that not only had the pickup broken down but it had also done so at a really inconvenient place. Continuing to enjoy the taste of my taco, I walked up to the pickup and was momentarily startled when I realized the person hunched over the hood inspecting the engine was a former student who, after finishing high school, had graduated from college and now worked as a high school principal. Ricardo looked up from the pickup and asked for help in getting his pickup running before the train arrived at the crossroad. I handed him the plate of food and encouraged him to eat as much as he wanted while I took on the task of fixing the pickup.

As the dream unfolded, I thought that I knew I could fix the pickup even though in my waking world, I was not mechanically inclined and would have no idea what to do. Sure enough, I quickly concluded the problem was the result of a faulty distributor cap, which kept the spark from getting to the pistons. With some slight adjustment to the distributor cap, the electrical connection was made, and the pickup started. It was now possible for my former student to drive the pickup off the railroad track.

As he prepared to drive away, Ricardo handed back a cleaned plate. I thanked him for the offer of a ride but knew in my heart that the reason for walking the highway was to become the big brother for others in need. Thanks to my big brother's help to fix my problems, I was now ready to help others. I was now the big brother.

CREEI SCORE: . . . . . **+?+?+//++?//++++**

ANTICIPATORY

When Eugene heard this dream, he knew immediately that Gene Schmidt had finished his work with the local school board and was ready to go onto another phase of life. He did move on to be superintendent of schools in another and larger New Mexico community not long thereafter.

Conclusion

We end by encouraging you to continue to practice THE CREEI PROCESS and play with it. As it touches your inner core you will learn better how it fits into your life and belief system. Using THE CREEI PROCESS is only an intermediate step to a better and more complete way for you to become integrated and whole.

THE CREEI PROCESS is hardly an end product etched in stone. We strongly encourage you to hold the TWELVE QUESTIONS carefully in your heart. Perhaps you will want to rephrase them to suit your own understanding of them, or add to them, or even replace one or more with a different question that speaks to your heart. Allow your heart to express itself while head respectfully listens. Sure, your head can and will have its say, too. Use this process as a portal to your inner meaning.

Our final word is a reflection on our experience of the process of creating this manual. Naturally we apply THE CREEI PROCESS. Right now here is how we would score it: **+++++//?++//++++** MOTIVATIONAL.

We score this experience this way because it is clear what we should be doing, we are responding to our inner needs by sharing it with you, we are expressing these words with great emotion of gratitude and love, and we are interacting with you through the medium of the printed word. It has been an extraordinarily pleasant experience to create this book, we feel safe in sharing it with you, our self-esteem is good, we have been authentic in what we have written, we feel confident that you the reader will grow as you experience this process, and we know that each of us has grown tremendously in the exercise of getting the words down as clearly as we can. Completeness is the only (**?**) as we write, but your act in holding these words in your hands and your hearts will be our completeness and make this a TRANSFORMATIVE experience. Thank you.

APPENDIXES

Appendix A

At this point, you've read the book and are no doubt well versed in THE CREEI PROCESS, and have probably worked several (at least one) of your own dreams.

How did it go? What kind of ahas did you have? Do you see what I saw about the brilliance (and sneakiness) of this technique?

OK, as promised in the forward of this book, I'll share with you the wretched dream I brought into the CREEI workshop, and what I did to change it into a sweet dream.

But, before I do, you should know that "changing the ending of the dream" is not necessarily a part of THE CREEI PROCESS, but is a technique I've developed over the past twenty years of professional dream work. Some would say that it resembles IRT (Imagery Rehearsal Therapy). My working premise is that there's no such thing as a bad dream because the dream isn't over until you've redirected it to an empowered conclusion. A nightmare (TRAUMATIC dream) is an unfinished dream. I believe it is incumbent upon the dreamer to act as director (or at least co-director) of his or her dream movie, and carry the dream through to its empowered conclusion. For example, if you have a nightmare and it ends abruptly just as you are jumping off the cliff, being cornered by wolves or your ass is hanging out in public, then it's your job to "finish the dream."

Thanks to the CREEI method for shining a laser beam of light on my dream, helping me to excavate it and bring it to the point where I was then able to "finish the dream" with greater ease and clarity.

Spoiler Alert: This dream has a little (OK, a lot) to do with my *derrière*.

Here is the dream:

Kelly Sullivan Walden

I'm observing a blonde woman (not me, by the way, but, of course, everyone in our dreams is us—and for me, any blonde person in my dream is a not-so-cryptic-code that it's really me) who is soon to be receiving an award, à la the Academy Awards.

She's wearing a gorgeous, bejeweled dress, and is giving partial acceptance speeches...all over the stage, in strange staccato ways. I, being omniscient, can see that there is a woman hidden at the edge of the stage, wearing a white dress and a headset, telling the blonde woman via her ear-prompter, where to go, what to say, when to turn and how to be.

I'm disgusted that this blonde woman is being bossed around like a perfect little soldier, except that it's not working! From the audience's perspective, she's completely disconnected.

Finally, it's time for her to receive her award. But, instead of presenting her with an award, she receives an even more gorgeous dress. She says thank you, and the woman with the headphone instructs her to put the dress on, so the blonde begins to look for a backstage changing room, only she can see that there is no backstage.

The headset lady instructs her to change right there.

The blonde questions her. "Right here? In front of everyone?"

Yes.

I know that the blonde is modest, and I watch her as she turns her back to the audience

and disrobes, and tries to wiggle into the dress...
only it's too small! And the dress gets stuck right
under her ass!

    The dream comes to a screeching halt when the
blonde woman says, "Are you fucking kidding me!?!"

CREEI SCORE: . . . . . **+-?+-//-??//??-+**

ANTICIPATORY-TRAUMATIC

For reasons that are probably too obvious to mention, I, Kelly, the dreamer, awoke feeling very upset. I was angry, shocked and off-center. As you know, if you read the forward to this book, this was the point where I met Eugene and THE CREEI PROCESS. After attending Eugene's workshop, here's the poem I wrote, to "finish" this dream:

NO IFS, ANDS OR BUTTS
My ass is hanging out on stage tonight
In front of everyone
my worst fear expressed
'cause I can't fit in my dress
I was supposed to be receiving an award
a reward for being a people pleaser *extraordinaire*
Fred Astaire
On air
Minus Ginger Rogers
'cause she's not there
she trying so hard to get it right
holding tight
to the rope she walks
trying so hard to do what she's been told,
trying so hard to not grow old
trying so hard to not be too bold
'cause they like you, won't love you
won't protect you, won't accept you, won't respect you

In fact, they'll reject you

but what the FUCK!
I did what they said,
I became the Walking Dead
I wore the pretty dress
they swore would look best
on me and my figure
now they'll have an image that's sure to linger
of me in my naked glory
wiggling into this ridiculous story
real quick before they can get a good look at my ass
real quick before they have time to ask
why not use a changing room?
or go backstage to a private womb?

Because there is no backstage,
not at this age!
It's all upfront
and there's nowhere to hide
so, you're forced to see my backside
and the moon, she's full tonight.
I'm stuck in a dress that doesn't fit
I'm stuck in my shame and it feels like....

My people pleasing is broken
That's it!
I quit
I'm out
I'm done
Whoever you are!
See my white flag
You've won!
I rip off the dress

Unzip my distress
Leave the scene of the crime just in time
Naked as a Blue Jay walking a fine line
Shake it all off
And then it hits me:
The worst thing happened
my public humiliation
my ass hanging out for all to see
but I'm not dead, it didn't kill me,
I'm still me, in fact more me
'cause now I have permission to be
surprised to suddenly be free
of the shackles that used to bind
me to the disease to please that made me blind
to the fact that I was in a Stepford trance

But, now I can do my own dance
to my own rhythm, my own grooves,
my own gyrations, and my own moves
I could end this dream here and I'd be fine.
but my stage of Shame is still behind,
I've got to go back and claim what's mine.
After all, it's my ass that's still on the line

I've got to figure out how to make it right
I've got to figure out how to plug into my light
if takes all night, and takes all of my might

Because how can I love if I'm not there
how can I contribute if I don't care?
I have to participate, to integrate, to excavate, to retaliate,
at least put in my two cents
Otherwise it's not worth wearing the most beautiful dress

I deserve this award
a reward for getting my ass back in my body
for honoring my soul
that's worth more than gold
In my acceptance speech, I'll share
about my glorious derrière
that was out there for all to see
And it didn't kill me
I'm still alive,
in fact, I thrive.

The experience of shining a light on this dream and turning it into rhyme has been one of the most empowering things I've ever done. As a result of this experience, I question anyone who feels the need to tell me what to do. In the past, I've been the type that people seem to feel at liberty to boss around—and because I'm a harmony-seeking being (aka "conflict avoidant"), I found it easier to go along with their program. Because of this, I've been praised for being "easy to work with," "lovable," "in the flow," which is not authentically how I always feel. As the poem indicates, I realized that if I truly want to contribute to people and love them in a genuine way, then I have to be myself and risk the pain of rejection. Rejection might sting, but it carries a far less consequence than the soullessness of being a people pleaser *extraordinaire*.

I love the saying, "Those who matter don't mind, and those who mind, don't matter." I figure, if people (my people) truly love me, they will put up with me being my authentic, uniquely expressed self—and maybe even celebrate it! At least I imagine they will prefer the real me over the fool's gold of my former Stepford persona. This dream process truly has transformed me, emboldened me and empowered me...in so many important ways. I'm truly grateful!

P.S. Here's a video of me performing this story/dream/poem just a few weeks after meeting Eugene at his CREEI workshop: https://tinyurl.com/noifsandsorbutts.

Appendix B

MORE SCORED DREAMS

Normally in a Dream Workshop or Seminar you the participant would be scoring your dream while getting feedback about the appropriateness of that scoring. This Appendix is intended to be a substitute for that. Here is how we scored a lot of our own dreams, arranged by their CREEI Pattern. These dreams are verbatim from our dream notebooks.

PATTERN 1 – TRANSFORMATIVE

Eugene

LEVITATION, September 11, 2015

> *I am with some people on what looks like a school playground. I meet Arnold Mindell, and we talk. Because of the subject that comes up (don't remember what it was), I pull out of my back pants pocket a paperback book on coma. At the same time, I stumble and fall to the ground on my knees. Arnold comes to my aid and lifts me up high over his head. He seems so strong. Then I stand up and begin to levitate, going up higher than nearby rooftops and beyond. Arnold motions to me to come back down to a particular spot.*

CREEI SCORE: . . . . . **+++++//+++//++++**

Why I scored it this way: The scene is clear, and I am involved with Arnold Mindell, founder of Process Work[36], a highly capable and

---

[36] https://www.processwork.edu/about-pwi/mission/

inspirational creative physicist/psychologist, and good friend with whom I am comfortable and who lifts me up higher than expected when I stumble. But he also brings me down to earth when I get too high. The entire episode is pleasant, safe, and self-esteem promoting. I feel totally free to be authentic and enjoy how all aspects and characters feel their beauty as I feel mine. It is clear that my friend Arnold is giving direction to move me toward my higher self in a wiser way than I had chosen, by which I feel comforted and confirmed.

Bob

TAKING CARE OF A PATIENT, September 25, 2015

I am in a clinic, modern but not my usual one. I am seeing a man with a skin rash of some sort. I diagnose it and suggest a number of treatments. I am happy to be taking care of him and to help him, and he is happy with the advice. At the last moment, I see some lines of crusty red skin two to three millimeters in width that look like body skin folds, which, in the course of the rash, have become secondarily infected, and so I tell him to use specifically on those areas the double antibiotic ointment. I am glad I caught my near omission.

CREEI SCORE: . . . . . **+++++//+++//++++**

Context: Bob had been on a three-month sabbatical from his medical practice and was not particularly looking forward to returning to work and facing the mountain of mail and numerous medication requests. He knew that once he got into that room with that patient, he would be okay, and it was tremendously helpful in returning and facing the burdens anticipated. This helped him to go back to work.

Why I scored it this way: The dream is clear, I am responding to the needs of the other dream characters, I have good emotions and expression, am interacting, and the dream seems complete. It is pleasant and safe, and I have good self-esteem, am authentic, and am *beloving* and becoming.

PATTERN 2 – MOTIVATIONAL

Eugene

FATHER SITS IN, September 30, 2015

In a classroom-like room with several men sitting in chairs of various designs with their backs against a wall. Gene England is in one of the chairs closest to the room entrance, perhaps the second chair. I am six or seven chairs farther from the door. As we all sit in silence, my father opens the door and comes into the room. I stand up quickly to offer him my spot, but he looks around first and then notices the empty chair where Gene England had just been and chooses that chair.

CREEI SCORE: . . . . . **+++?+//+++//++++**

Why I scored it this way: The room in the dream is only partially clear and my interaction with everyone is not clear or resolved. Nevertheless, the action of my father taking the seat left by long time deeply respected best friend Gene England instead of the one I have offered him seems immediately resolving, empowering and comforting to me. The dream is complete, I am safe, it is pleasant, my self-esteem is high, I am being authentic, beloving and am moving toward my higher self.

Bob

BEGONIA STORE, December 29, 2013

I am in a small shop that sells plants—not different kinds of plants but only begonias. But I see many, many kinds of begonias. A woman is actually selling the leaves; I see a whole wall of a rack with all kinds of begonia leaves of various

shades of green with various shades of yellows,
reds, and other colors. The situation is that we
would buy a leaf and she showed us how you make
small cuts in the leaf and then put soil on top of it
and it forms into the living begonia plant. I have
not had success with this before but want to try it.
The shopkeeper is a pretty woman in her fifties, a
nice person.

CREEI Score: . . . . . **+++?+//+++//++++**

Context: Bob discussed this dream with Eugene, and it turned out that his wife, Birgitta, knew exactly how to do this. Later, she taught him how to do it. Before the dream, he had no idea that this could be done!

Why I scored it this way: The scene is clear and easy to describe. My role in shopping for and wanting to grow begonias is clear. My emotional energy is high as I am enthused about the begonias, but I am not sure I am expressing that well. I interact with the shopkeeper and the begonias, and the episode seems complete. It is pleasant, I am safe my esteem is high, I am being my authentic self, the begonias experience their own beauty, and I am becoming a better person.

PATTERN 3 — ANTICIPATORY

Bob

RAINSTORM, July 27, 2014

My wife and I are high on a hill in a city—on
an empty street with no traffic. The sky is overcast,
and it is raining. We can see far below us to the east
where a couple of young women are swimming in
an area that appears to have been made by the rain
runoff. They are having fun with the swimming.
They are too far away for us to be able to tell who
they are. At one point, they are holding on to a rope

and being pulled upstream; this looks potentially
dangerous to me because they are being pulled
rapidly toward a concrete structure. They are okay,
but it starts to rain harder and harder. It gets to
raining so hard at times that I cannot see my wife,
who is only ten feet away from me. But somehow the
rain is not bothering us. We are not getting cold or
uncomfortable, and it is an exciting thing.

CREEI SCORE: . . . . . **+?++?//+++//++?+**

Why I scored it this way: The scene is clear, but it is not clear what my role was. I was not really reacting to the situation but was merely observing it. My emotional energy is high, and I am expressing my energies, but I am not interacting much with the situation. It seems to come to a conclusion. It was, all in all, pleasant, and my wife and I were safe. I had good self-worth and was being authentic in experiencing the situation. It is not clear, since I was not interacting well, whether other dream characters (wife, two young women, the rain) were experiencing their own beauty, but I was growing as an individual.

PATTERN 4 – TRAUMATIC

Eugene

MASTER'S DEGREE, August 24, 2015

I am in a construction site in a nuclear
technology-related area, where I see a
few buildings amid chaos and debris. My
assignment is to organize/coordinate the several
multidisciplinary professionals at this facility who
are not sure what the objective of this project is but
who are highly capable in their own disciplines.
I understand I am to receive a master's degree
if I succeed, even though I announce that I
already have a PhD in research from long ago. I

understand that this project is a practical one, not research oriented. One man, a competent designer, goes about his business in a methodical way, and I overhear him mention having to meet with his bishop. I assume from this that he is Mormon. He has made an office out of a vacant room in one of the buildings. Later, he has invited me to go somewhere with him in his car, but before taking off, he lights up a cigarette stub. This surprises me, and I ask to get out of the car since I don't like to be around that kind of smoke.

CREEI SCORE: . . . . . **+++++//−?+//+?−+**

Context: This dream happened the night after my first meeting with Los Alamos Faith and Science Forum's Steering Committee.

Why I scored it this way: The dream is clear enough, although some of the debris and chaos are not something I could sketch. My role in it is clear, which I accept with a high feeling of confidence and challenge and express to all those in the dream with whom I interact. The scene is neither resolved nor totally pleasant because I do not feel beloving of one particular professional. It occurred to me in scoring that I need to work on how to relate to the professionals I am assigned to in a beloving, motivating way despite the habits or aspects of some that displease me.

Bob

MOUNTAIN ROAD, March 8, 2013

I am driving a four-wheel-drive car on a mountain road that I have driven before and often use. I come around a corner and see that the road ahead is not good, much less maintained than I remembered. I stop to look at it and am concerned about slipping off. I also think that if I had used my momentum instead of stopping, it would have been much better—that stopping had made it more difficult to maneuver. It was good to have stopped, but it potentially made it worse.

CREEI SCORE: . . . . . **+++++//--?//???+**

Why I scored it this way: The story is clear. My role as a driver is clear, and my emotion is high. I am expressing my emotion as I think through the problem, and I am expressing that in my decision-making. I am interacting with the road and car, but the situation was woefully incomplete. It was not pleasant, and I did not feel safe. My self-esteem was questioned as a driver, but I was my authentic self in judging the situation. The other characters (road, car) were not much appreciated by me and so could not be called exactly beloved, but I was in the process of becoming a more skilled and practiced driver.

PATTERNS 3&4 – ANTICIPATORY-TRAUMATIC

Eugene

ROUND TABLE FURY, May 11, 1965

I am with Mother and Father at a small round dinner table, conversing. I begin to talk about a subject that gets Dad's interest, and he encourages me to say more. As I respond, eager to continue, Mother interrupts with a disapproving comment that makes me furious, so furious that I no longer want to discuss anything and all I can do is glower at her.

CREEI SCORE: . . . . . **+?++?//-?+//?+?+**

Why I scored it this way: The dream is clear. However, my behavior is both responsive and reactive, which means my responsiveness (respondability) is uncertain. My emotion is definitely high, as is my expression, even when I become silent, since my negative expression is obvious in my face and body. Interaction is mixed between Father (who had passed on the year before) and Mother (still alive); thus, I am interacting differently to both at the same time. The dream is certainly not complete, resolved, or satisfying. My behavior is both pleasant to Dad but not so to Mother; thus, the overall score is uncertain. Yes, to feeling safe. I'm uncertain about the feeling of high self-esteem, especially in my attitude toward Mother, the score of which is also reflected in the eleventh question on beloving. Even though my behavior toward Father and Mother are different in the dream, it is nevertheless authentic. In terms of "becoming," a clear lesson can be learned from my reaction, so that is why I have scored (+) rather than procrastinating.

Eugene

LAWRENE'S SUPPORT, March 1966

> *At a corral-like place, outside the wooden fence. The woman (in the previous scene) is alone and inside in a position of standing to speak or preach to those on the outside of the fence. There seems to be a barn or stable nearby available to her. I am aware of people gathered near the fence near me. She is talking about spirituality, responding with statements that those who talk of spiritual experience in that way are fakes. Then I proceed to ask penetrating questions, direct and even angry questions. Those around are startled at the bluntness. Those who once clapped are now stunned. I am alone and in pain, but know I must proceed with brutal questioning to be true to my convictions and sense of duty. Suddenly, I become aware of arms flung around my midriff from behind. It is Lawrene! (Eugene's second wife) She is with me. My strength and courage increase.*

CREEI SCORE: . . . . . **+?+++//+?+//++??**

ANTICIPATORY-TRAUMATIC

The context: This dream came well before THE CREEI PROCESS was invented in 1987 and near the beginning of Eugene's awareness of the importance of dreams as a mechanism for evaluating one's personal behavior.

Why I scored it this way: The dream is clear, since it is easy to describe. My role is assertive, but reactionary and needs reexamination in light of questions 2 and 11. My emotion (passion) is obviously high, and I am expressing it fully. My interaction with others is high, and I have a sense of completion when Lawrene comes into the scene. Nevertheless, the pleasantness of the scene is questionable because it is both pleasant and unpleasant. My sense of safety is high, because I have no fear. My sense of self-esteem is high—perhaps too high! And I am being authentic, even though not everyone in the scene feels their beauty in my presence, especially the woman I am challenging. This is the aspect I needed to reexamine carefully, not only for this dream but in my outer general behavior. Nevertheless, despite my inner sense of purpose, I am not sure I'm becoming closer to my highest self.

Eugene

HIGH FLYING, January 18, 1966

Scene 1. Earthquake

I've parked my motorcycle outside, but am near the apartment building where Betty and her mother live. I see abandoned concrete buildings nearby built on the side, and on top of hills, one of which has a tall smoke stack. I am in one. Suddenly, I experience much lurching. Seems like an earthquake. I'm not frightened but powerless to move on my own from out of the building. Others in the building wonder what is going on. We just stick with it until we can get out of building.

CREEI SCORE: . . . . . **?+++?//--?//++??**

ANTICIPATORY-TRAUMATIC

Scene 2. The Push-Pull

Once out of the building, I feel a kind of "magnetic" pull in a certain direction. I am being pulled toward rolling hills, barren-looking hills. I accept the pull and start moving in its direction, but then stumble. As I put my hands out to break my fall, I find myself beginning to fly! Then I discover that by having my hands out a little to the sides and turning them properly as a sort of rudder, I can control my flying. It is a delicate movement of hands that controls flight. Too much and I go too high too fast. Others are below me now. They are being pulled backward as if they are trying to fight the pull.

I shout to try to gain their attention. No one hears. I am passing some up. Near me are some telephone or power lines; I come in contact with a single strand. I grab hold, but I am not affected (hurt). (It is covered with black frayed insulation.) I turn a summersault over the wire. Now I'm trying to stay as close to ground as possible. Not yet greatly skilled at this. Not afraid. I am curious but lonely.

CREEI SCORE: . . . . . **++++?//?++//++?+**

MOTIVATIONAL

Comment: This scene scores differently than Scene 1, but are here together to highlight that different scenes do not necessarily have the same pattern.[37] This Scene 2 is MOTIVATIONAL, near ANTICIPATORY, but certainly not TRAUMATIC.

Context: Near the apartment or home of Betty, Eugene's first wife from whom he was estranged. Her mother lives there too.

---

[37] It was with this dream that I decided to score dreams scenes separately, because it became clear that scores might be different.

Why I scored it this way: I have found that it is useful to score each scene separately because the difference in scores can show trends. Scene 1 is not as clear as scene 2. Just that small difference is interesting in answering the first CREEI question on clarity. The high scores for respondability, emotion, and expression, as well as the uncertain scores are essentially the same in both scenes. However, completion is lower in scene 1 than 2. The trend in the dream is toward resolution or completion, if not satisfaction, as the dream proceeds. All the other questions score the same in both scenes, namely high in pleasantness, safety, self-esteem, authenticity, and becoming. Only beloving is uncertain, because it is not clear to my dream self how other characters are experiencing themselves. Whatever they are experiencing does not seem to have anything to do with my own behavior in the dream.

Appendix C

DREAMS FROM SIGMUND FREUD

B elow are five of seven dreams from Sigmund Freud's pioneering book *The Interpretation of Dreams*.[38]

Sigmund Freud

GOETHE ATTACKS HERR M.,[39] undated

> *One of my acquaintances, Herr M., had been attacked in an essay with an unjustifiable degree of violence, as we all thought—by no less a person than Goethe. Herr M. was naturally crushed by the attack. He complained of it bitterly to some company at table; his veneration for Goethe had not been affected, however, by the chronological data, which seemed to me improbable. Goethe died in 1832. Since his attack on Herr M. must have been quite naturally have been made earlier that that, Herr M. must have been quite a young man at the time. It seemed to be sure, however, what year we were actually in, so that my whole calculation melted into obscurity. Incidentally, the attack was contained in Goethe's well-known essay on "Nature."*

CREEI SCORE: . . . . . **+??−+//−−?//?+?−**

ANTICIPATORY-TRAUMATIC

---

[38] See Chapter 6 for the first two dreams, which are summarized in **Spreadsheet 5**.
[39] Ibid. 475-7

PORTAL TO MEANING

117

Sigmund Freud
CROWD OF PEOPLE,[40] undated

After his death, my father played a political part among the Magyars and brought them together politically. Here I saw a small and indistinct picture: a crowd of men as though they were in the Reichstag; someone standing on one or two chairs, with other people 'round him. I remembered how like Garibaldi he had looked on his death-bed, and felt glad that that promise had come true.

CREEI SCORE: . . . . . **??+−−//+++//++??**

ANTICIPATORY

Sigmund Freud
NEWS OF SON FROM THE FRONT,[41] undated

I said to my wife that I had a piece of news for her, something quite special. She was alarmed and refused to listen. I assured her that on the contrary it was something that she would be glad to hear, and began to tell her that our son's officer's mess had sent a sum of money (5,000 Kronen?)... something about distinction... distribution.... Meanwhile I had gone with her into a small room, like a storeroom, to look for something. Suddenly I saw my son appear. He was not in uniform but in tight-fitting sports clothes (like a seal?), with a little cap. He climbed up on to a basket that was standing beside a cupboard, as though he wanted to put something on the cupboard. I called out to him: no reply. It seemed to me that his face

---

[40] Ibid. 363
[41] Ibid. 597 The ellipses are from the original text.

*or forehead was bandaged. He was adjusting
something in his mouth, pushing something into
it. And his hair was flecked with grey. I thought:
"Could he be as exhausted as all that? And has
he got false teeth?" Before I could call out again
I woke up, feeling no anxiety but with my heart
beating rapidly.*

CREEI

SCORE: . . . . . +++++//−−+//?+?+ TRAUMATIC

Sigmund Freud

RUNNING UPSTAIRS UNDRESSED,[42] undated

*I was incompletely dressed and was going
upstairs from a flat on the ground floor to a higher
story. I was going up three steps at a time and was
delighted at my agility. Suddenly I saw a maid-
servant coming down the stairs—coming towards
me, that is. I felt ashamed and tried to hurry,
and at this point the feeling of being inhibited set
in: I was glued to the steps and unable to budge
from the spot.*

CREEI SCORE: . . . . . **+?+?−//−?+//?+??**

ANTICIPATORY-TRAUMATIC

Sigmund Freud

RIDING ON A HORSE,[43] undated

*I was riding on a grey horse, timidly and
awkwardly to begin with, as though I were only
reclining upon it. I met one of my colleagues,
P., who was sitting high on a horse, dressed in*

---

[42] Ibid. 272
[43] Ibid., 263.

a tweed suit, and who drew my attention to something (probably to my bad seat). I now began to find myself sitting more and more firmly and comfortably on my highly intelligent horse, and noticed that I was feeling quite at home up there. My saddle was a kind of bolster, which completely filled the space between its neck and crupper. In this way, I rode straight in between two vans. After riding some distance up the street, I turned 'round and tried to dismount, first in front of a small open chapel that stood in the street frontage. Then I actually did dismount in front of another chapel that stood near it. My hotel was in the same street; I might have let the horse go to it on its own, but I preferred to lead it there. It was as though I should have felt ashamed to arrive at it on horseback. A hotel 'boots' was standing in front of the hotel; he showed me a note of mine that had been found, and laughed at me over it. In the note was written, doubly underlined: "No food" and then another remark (indistinct) such as "No work," together with a vague idea that I was in a strange town in which I was doing no work.

CREEI SCORE: . . . . . **+++−?//−?+//?+?+**

ANTICIPATORY-TRAUMATIC

If Freud had had the summary of the CREEI scans as in **Spreadsheet 5** he might have seen clearly several trends. First, all of these dreams were clear. Obviously, Freud remembered his dreams in detail. And it is not surprising that in all of these dreams he had good self-esteem. But did he realize how seldom it was that he scored (+) in Responsiveness, Emotion, Expressing, Interaction, Authenticity and Becoming? Especially convicting is that in none of the nine dreams did he score (+) in *beloving*.

We can only speculate about what Freud's heart was trying desperately to communicate to him about how his patients, friends, colleagues, and reading public might have viewed him. He was evidently not in the habit of *beloving* others, at least not in how he behaved in his dreams. Instead of labeling these dreams as absurd he might have learned some things about himself.

Appendix D

DREAMS FROM LEO TOLSTOY

In his magnificent novel, *War and Peace*, Leo Tolstoy used dreams a few times to demonstrate what was happening in the mind of the character. He used this device sparingly, but effectively.

(Note that in the following quotations we have used italics for dream segments consistent with other dreams in this book. We have also created the names of the dreams.)

At one point, Pierre Bezukhov, one of the main characters, records in his journal the following three dreams:

Dreamer	DateDrmd	Title	C	R	E	E	I	//	C	P	S	//	E	A	B	B	Ch1	Ch2	Ptn	Notes
PB	N/A	Three Dogs	+	-	+	+	-	//	-	+	+	//	+	+	?	+	BroA		3,4	
PB	N/A	Questionable Affection	+	+	+	-	?	//	?	?	?	//	?	?	?	?	IA		4	
PB	N/A	Song of Songs	+	+	+	+	?	//	?	+	+	//	+	+	+	+	IA		2	
AB	N/A	Death comes to Prince Andrei	+	+	+	+	+	//	+	+	+	//	+	+	+	+	N		4?	
NAB	N/A	Nicolenka's Dream	+	?	+	+	?	//	-	?	?	//	?	?	?	+	NB	NI	3,4	

Spreadsheet 8. Dreams from Leo Tolstoy's novel War and Peace.

Pierre Bezukhov

(Fictional character in novel War and Peace)

THREE DOGS!,[44] undated

> *I dreamed that I was walking in the darkness
> and was suddenly surrounded by dogs, but I
> walked on without fear; suddenly one small dog
> seized my left thigh with its teeth and would not
> let go. I began to strangle it with my hands. And
> I had only just torn it off when another bigger
> one seized me by the chest. I tore that one off, but
> a third, still bigger, began to bite me. I started to
> lift it up, but the more I lifted it, the bigger and
> heavier it became. And suddenly brother A. came
> and, taking me by the arm, led me with him and
> brought me to a building, to enter which one had
> to pass over a narrow plank. I stepped on it, and
> the plank bent and fell, and I started climbing up
> a fence which I could barely reach with my hands.
> With great effort, I dragged myself over it in such
> a way that my legs hung on one side and my body
> on the other. I turned and saw that brother A.
> was standing on the fence and pointing out to me
> a big avenue and garden, and in the garden a big
> beautiful building. I woke up.*

CREEI SCORE: . . . . . **+−++−//−−−//++?+**

ANTICIPATORY-TRAUMATIC

---

[44] Tolstoy, 443-444.

Pierre Bezukhov

QUESTIONABLE AFFECTION,[45] undated

Dreamed that Iosif Alexeevich was sitting in my house, and I was very glad and wanted to make him welcome. That I was babbling incessantly with other people and suddenly remembered that he would not like it, and I wanted to get close to him and embrace him. But as soon as I got close to him, I saw that his face was transfigured, had become young, and he was telling me something very, very softly about the teaching of the order, so softly that I couldn't hear it. That we all left the room, and then something complicated happened. We were sitting or lying on the floor. He was saying something to me. And I wanted to show him my sensitivity, and, without listening to what he said, I began to imagine to myself the state of my inner man and the grace of God coming upon me. And tears came to my eyes, and I was pleased that he noticed it But he looked at me with vexation and jumped up, breaking off his conversation I grew timid and asked whether what he was saying referred to me; but he did not reply, looked at me gently, and after that we were suddenly in my bedroom, where there was a double bed He lay on the edge of it, and I, as if burning with the desire to caress him, lay beside him. And he asked me: "Tell me truly, what is your main predilection? Do you know it? I think you've already found it out." Embarrassed by this question, I replied that laziness was my main predilection. He shook his head mistrustfully. And,

---

[45] Ibid, 444-445.

still more embarrassed, I replied that, though I
was living with my wife on his advice, I was not
a husband to my wife. To this he objected that my
wife should not be deprived of my caresses, and
gave me to understand that this was my duty. But
I replied that I was ashamed of it; and suddenly
everything disappeared.

And I woke up and found in my thoughts
the text of Holy Scripture: "And the life was the
light of men. And the light shineth in the darkness
and the darkness comprehended it not." Iosif
Alexeevich's face had been youthful and bright.
That day I received a letter from my benefactor
about the duty of married life.

CREEI SCORE: . . . . . **+++++//??+//?++?**

TRAUMATIC

Pierre Bezukhov

SONG OF SONGS,[46] undated

Had a dream from which I awakened with a
pounding heart.

I dreamed that I was in Moscow, in my own
house, in the big sitting room, and Iosif Alexeevich
came out of the drawing room. That I recognized
him at once that the process of rebirth had already
been accomplished with him, and I rushed to meet
him. That I kissed him and his hands, and he
said: "Have you noticed that I now have a different
face?" I looked at him, still holding him in my
embrace, and saw that his face was young, but
there was no hair on his head and his features were
quite different. And that I said to him: "I would

---

[46] Ibid., 444-445.

recognize you if I met you by chance"—and at the
same time I thought: "Was I telling the truth?"
And suddenly I saw that he was lying there like a
dead body; then he gradually recovered and went
with me into a big study, holding a big book written
on royal paper. And I said: "I wrote this." And he
answered me by inclining his head. I opened the
book, and there were beautiful pictures on all the
pages. And I knew that these pictures represented
the amorous adventures of a soul with its beloved.
And I saw on the pages a beautiful image of a girl in
transparent clothing and with a transparent body,
flying up to the clouds. And I knew that this girl
was none other than the image of the Song of Songs.
And looking at these pictures, I felt that I was doing
a bad thing, and I could not tear myself away from
them. Lord, help me! My God, if Thy forsaking of
me is Thy doing, then Thy will be done; but if I
myself am the cause of it, then teach me what to do.
I will perish of my own depravity if Thou forsake
me altogether.

CREEI SCORE: . . . . . **+++++//?++//++++**
MOTIVATIONAL

Tolstoy is having Pierre judge himself, doing an injustice to himself, instead of loving his dream. Pierre lets his head get in the way of his heart. How would the story have been different if he had done THE CREEI PROCESS and valued the dream? Of course, we think Pierre would have done much differently. It is interesting to observe that Tolstoy presents these three dreams as evolution from an ANTICIPATORY-TRAUMATIC dream to ANTICIPATORY to near TRANSFORMATIVE. It is probably the effect Tolstoy was striving to describe in his character.

The following shows how Tolstoy uses the device of a dream to describe what was happening in the mind of Prince Andrei a few days before his death.

Prince Andrei Bolkonsky

DEATH COMES TO PRINCE ANDREI,[47] undated

"In a dream, he saw himself lying in the same room in which he lay in reality, but he was not wounded, but healthy. Many sorts of persons, insignificant, indifferent, appear before Prince Andrei. He talks with them, argues about something unnecessary. They are preparing to go somewhere. Prince Andrei vaguely recalls that it is all insignificant and that he has other, more important concerns, but he goes on, to their surprise, speaking some sort of empty, witty words. Gradually, imperceptibly, all these people begin to disappear, and everything is replaced by the one question of the closed door. He gets up and goes to the door to slide the bolt and lock it. Everything depends on whether he does or does not manage to lock it. He walks, he hurries, his feet do not move, and he knows that he will not manage to lock the door, but still he painfully strains with all his force. And a tormenting fear seizes him. And this fear is the fear of death: it is standing behind the door. But as he is crawling strengthlessly and awkwardly toward the door, this terrible something is already pushing against it from the other side, forcing it. Something inhuman—death—is forcing the door, and he has to hold it shut. He lays hold of the door, strains in a last effort—to lock it is already impossible— just to hold it shut; but his

---

[47] Ibid., 984-5.

attempts are weak, clumsy, and, pushed by the terrible thing, the door keeps opening and shutting again. Once more it pushes from the other side, his last supernatural efforts are in vain, and the two halves open noiselessly. It comes in, and it is death. And Prince Andrei died.

"But in the same instant that he died, Prince Andrei remembered that he was asleep, and in the same instant that he died, he made an effort with himself and woke up.

"Yes, that was death. I died—I woke up. Yes, death is an awakening." Clarity suddenly came to his soul, and the curtain that until then had concealed the unknown was raised before his inner gaze. He felt the release of a force that previously had been as if bound in him and that strange lightness which from then on did not leave him.

"When, having come to in a cold sweat, he stirred on his sofa, Natasha went over to him and asked what was the matter. He did not answer, and not understanding her, gave her a strange look.

"That was what had happened to him two days before Princess Marya's arrival. Since that day, the doctor said, the wasting fever had taken a turn for the worse, but Natasha was not interested in what the doctor said: she saw those dreadful moral signs, which were more unquestionable for her.

"Since that day, there began Prince Andrei, along with his awakening from sleep, an awakening from life. And it seemed no slower to him, in relation to the length of life, than an awakening from sleep in relation to the length of a dream."

This was too hard for authors to score as it was translated from Russian. But when Bob discovered it could be scored more easily if the translation were put in first person, present tense, he realized we were on to something!

Initially we had a difficult time applying THE CREEI PROCESS to this dream. Then we transformed the description of the dream into the first person, present tense and it came out as follows:

Prince Andrei Bolkonsky
DEATH COMES TO PRINCE ANDREI
(RETOLD IN FIRST PERSON, PRESENT TENSE)[48] undated

I see myself lying in the same room in which I lay in reality, but I am not wounded, but healthy. Many sorts of persons, insignificant, indifferent, appear before me. I talk with them, argue about something unnecessary. They are preparing to go somewhere. I vaguely recall that it is all insignificant and that I have other, more important concerns, but I go on, to their surprise, speaking some sort of empty, witty words. Gradually, imperceptibly, all these people begin to disappear, and everything is replaced by the one question of the closed door. I get up and go to the door to slide the bolt and lock it. Everything depends on whether I do or do not manage to lock it. I walk, I hurry, my feet do not move, and I know that I will not manage to lock the door, but still I painfully strain all my force. And a tormenting fear seizes me. And this fear is the fear of death: it is standing behind the door. But as I am crawling strengthlessly and awkwardly toward the door, this terrible something is already pushing against it from the other side, forcing it. Something

---

[48] Ibid., 984-5. Retold by us in the first person

inhuman—death—is forcing the door, and I have
to hold it shut. I lay hold of the door, strain in a
last effort—to lock it is already impossible—just
to hold it shut; but my attempts are weak, clumsy,
and, pushed by the terrible thing, the door keeps
opening and shutting again.

Once more it pushes from the other side, my
last supernatural efforts are in vain, and the two
halves open noiselessly. It comes in, and it is death.
And I die.

CREEI SCORE: . . . . . **+++?+//+‐‐//++?+**
TRAUMATIC

Now the scoring is not so difficult.

Tolstoy remarkably demonstrates the process of working with a dream. The dream had been TRAUMATIC, but Prince Andrei has a revelation that changes it to a TRANSFORMATIVE dream by altering the appearance of death from unpleasant to pleasant, from unsafe to safe, and by realizing the beauty of death rather than its ugliness.

In one of the closing paragraphs of the novel, Prince Andrei's now fifteen-year-old son, Nikolai Bolkonsky,[49] has a dream:

Nikolai Andreyevich Bolkonsky

NIKOLENKA'S DREAM,[50] undated

Nikolenka, having just woken up in a cold
sweat, his eyes wide open, sat up on his bed and
looked around. A terrible dream had awakened
him. In his dream, he had seen himself and Pierre
wearing helmets—the kind illustrated in his
edition of Plutarch. He and Uncle Pierre were
marching at the head of a huge army. This army

---

[49] Nikolenka is the diminutive for Nikolai Andreiyevich Bolkonsky (Prince Andrei's son).
[50] Tolstoy, 1177.

*consisted of slanting white lines that filled the air
like the spider webs that fly about in the fall and
that Dessales called 'Le fil de la Vierge.*[51] *Ahead
was glory, just the same as these threads, only
slightly denser. They—he and Pierre—were racing
lightly and joyfully nearer and nearer to their
goal. Suddenly the threads that moved them began
to weaken, to tangle; the going became heavy. And
Uncle Nikolai Ilyich stood before them in a stern
and menacing pose.*

*"Did you do that?" he said, pointing to
the broken-up wax and pens. "I loved you, but
Arakcheev has given me orders, and I'll kill the
first one who moves forward." Nikolenka turned
to look at Pierre; but there was no longer any
Pierre. Pierre was his father, Prince Andrei, and
his father had no image or form, but he was there,
and, seeing him, Nikolenka felt weak from love:
he felt strengthless, boneless, and liquid. His father
caressed and pitied him. But Uncle Nikolai Ilyich
moved closer and closer to them. Nikolenka was
overcome by terror and woke up."*

We had the same trouble scoring from the third person. Here is that same dream transposed into first person format.

Nikolai Andreyevich Bolkonsky
NIKOLENKA'S DREAM,[52] undated
(Retold in the first person, present tense.)
*I see myself and Pierre wearing helmets—
the kind illustrated in his edition of Plutarch.
Uncle Pierre and I are marching at the head of a*

---

[51] "The thread of the Virgin."
[52] Ibid., 1177. Retold by us in the first person.

huge army. This army consists of slanting white lines that fill the air like the spider webs that fly about in the fall and that Dessales called 'Le fil de la Vierge'. Ahead is glory, just the same as these threads, only slightly denser. Pierre and I are racing lightly and joyfully nearer and nearer to our goal. Suddenly the threads that move us begin to weaken, to tangle; the going becomes heavy. And Uncle Nikolai Ilyich stands before us in a stern and menacing pose.

"Did you do that?" he says, pointing to the broken-up wax and pens. "I loved you, but Arakcheev has given me orders, and I'll kill the first one who moves forward." I turn to look at Pierre; but there is no longer any Pierre. Pierre is now my father, Prince Andrei, and he has no image or form, but he is there, and, seeing him, I feel weak from love: I feel strengthless, boneless, and liquid. My father caresses and pities me. But Uncle Nikolai Ilyich moves closer and closer to us. I am overcome by terror and wake up."

CREEI Score: . . . . . **+?+++//−??//?+?+**

<small>ANTICIPATORY-TRAUMATIC</small>

This is clearly a nightmare dream, but when Nikolenka awakens, his main engagement with the dream is the realization that it was his father, Prince Andrei, who was caressing him and approving of him, and Pierre as well. It was an inspiration to Nikolenka to strive for great things as he loved his father and Pierre. Here again, Tolstoy works with the dream and transforms it. This is a good example of the assumption presented early in this book: peace and joy can be found in any dream no matter how TRAUMATIC it might be.

Appendix E

Since CREEI was first developed in 1987, various participants in Dream Workshops and Seminars have written brief accounts of how CREEI influenced their lives. A few of these are included here in chronological order with permission of the authors, so that you, the reader, can have a better feel for what CREEI can do for you.

ROBERT A. REES, PhD
ADMINISTRATOR AT UCLA, LOS ANGELES, CA.
(This letter was from administrator Robert Rees regarding Eugene Kovalenko's UCLA course on dreams. Although CREEI was developed in 1987, this letter is an important antecedent.)

December 7, 1976

[TO:] Harold P. Fetter, Jr., D.D.S.,
Monterey Park, California

Dear Mr. Fetter:
Thank you for your letter of November 24, and for letting us know of your enthusiasm for Eugene Kovalenko's course on Creative Dreaming and Spiritual Awakening. You are one of many students who have found Dr. Kovalenko's course exciting and informative. I am particularly pleased with your enthusiastic report of your experience in Eugene's class since he is a close personal friend and I have long been an admirer of his ability to communicate with sincerity and force. We hope to schedule Dr. Kovalenko for other courses in the future.
Cordially,
Robert A. Rees, PhD, Director

Department of Humanities and Communications
University of California at Los Angeles

JOSEPH DILLARD, PhD
PSYCHOTHERAPIST, BERLIN, GERMANY
(FORMERLY IN PHOENIX, ARIZONA)

It is rare to find a hard-nosed engineer who will do more than sneer at his dreams. It is even more unusual to find one who is not only an enthusiastic and devoted dream researcher, but who has that rare and precious ability to translate difficult and obscure insights into practical, useful tools for the business world. Eugene Kovalenko, PhD, a materials scientist/engineer, international trade specialist and management consultant (who also happens to be a poet and talented baritone), has devised an ingeniously simple dream questionnaire, which has been used to increase productivity and improve employee relations in California companies. In addition, Dr. Kovalenko's methodology, called THE CREEI PROCESS, has received an enthusiastic reception by several groups of Soviet scientists and researchers in Kiev, before the fall of the USSR.

CREEI stands for the five dimensions by which the dreamer scores his nighttime creations in terms of questions about the clarity, role, emotion, expression and interaction of the dreamer in the dream. These questions, which can be answered yes, no or uncertain, are then related to a specific work issue with which the worker is concerned. The insight and practical usefulness which often bursts forth is surprisingly profound and mysteriously synchronous in its expression. Dr. Kovalenko's innovative techniques for bridging the inner world of intuition and creativity with the outer world of hard-nosed business acumen deserves the attention of both dream researchers and executives who want to improve employee relations, reduce stress-related absences and increase worker creativity.

Lou Avitable
Wintec Production Manager, Brunswick Defense Corporation

Indeed, life has its ups and downs but your method of self-examination has helped me improve my well-being. The positive direction that I took and the continuing upward direction of my life can be directly attributed to using your clever CREEI Process. I am fortunate and truly appreciate having been one of your first pupils.

Michael Jackson
Wintec General Manager, Brunswick Defense Corporation

This letter acknowledges the fact that the application of THE CREEI PROCESS concepts will play a major role in resolving interpersonal/personal conflicts. This was demonstrated in late 1987 in an actual case history involving an adverse working relationship between two department managers who, in early years, had worked exceedingly well together. The process provided a medium where the parties were better able to express and analyze both their interpersonal and personal conflicts and to effect changes positive to the organization and their personal lives. I am a believer in the potential power of the concept and feel that major improvements have been made this past year toward the development of a more formalized program by its founder, Eugene Kovalenko.

Nancy J. Swenson
Psychologist at Washington State Penitentiary

(Nancy Swenson had never been to a CREEI workshop but received materials about it from a friend. She found it useful and asked for Eugene's permission to use CREEI. This shows that that the personal participation of Eugene, originator of the process, was not necessary in a live workshop, as was initially believed.)

I am a staff psychologist, master's level, at the Washington Corrections Center in Shelton, Washington. I deal with male inmates only. I also have a small private practice in the community which specializes in Adult Children of Alcoholics and other dysfunctional families. In this setting, I counsel women in groups. In both settings, I have been trying to implement our [CREEI] process. It makes sense and is easy for all of my clients to use. Although we don't use it specifically to address job-related issues, I try to use a more universal approach and encourage them to see their lives as their jobs. I have not used it extensively. I have only used it enough to see if it is a feasible method to help my clients. It is.

RAUL G.
FORMER GANG MEMBER IN LOS ANGELES, CALIFORNIA

In my past experience, dreams have always been an inconvenience and a hindrance to what closing my eyes were all about: getting a good night's sleep. If there was anything I remembered from a night's sleep, it was always fear of a nightmare. It was with this skepticism that I was introduced to THE CREEI PROCESS and its founder, Eugene Kovalenko, who taught me how to:

1. Deal with and face my dreams
2. Transform my nightmares into optimistic outlooks
3. Benefit from the creative energy of my dreams.

All the preceding has resulted in a change of attitude and enlightened feelings to what comes each night when my eyes close. I look forward to wherever my mind and feelings will take me. Each night a new thought, experience and adventure takes place. A skeptic no more, I believe THE CREEI PROCESS has helped me tap into one of the greatest hidden sources of creative and self-realization available to us. THE CREEI PROCESS, when used properly, is the key to opening this door.

STEVE HERBRUCK
CEO, HERBRUCK'S RESEARCH. INC.

Dr. Kovalenko introduced THE CREEI PROCESS to me by using it during our first conversation. Nothing short of personal revelation overcame me instantly. All my life I have pondered the possibility of dreams being an integral part of our real lives. When something feels right and makes logical sense, I adopt it into my life. CREEI is the missing link to the eight hours of each night I spend in my mind's eye. The practical application of this process has given me the confidence, direction and emotional health I have longed for since childhood. I am so convinced that CREEI will have the same positive results on anyone who learns to use it that I have bought a part of the company. CREEI is a logical way to process one's hidden emotional realities that we act out only in our dreams. As you use it, you will naturally enlighten yourself about unresolved personal issues and find emotional balance. I hope that you will enjoy learning about your inner self as much as I have.

W. CLARK REX, PhD
CONSULTING BEHAVIORAL SCIENTIST,
    CEO, HOT SECTION TECHNOLOGIES, INC.

I have been using THE CREEI PROCESS for many years. I was intrigued with the process the first time Dr. Eugene Kovalenko explained it to me in the early 1990s and have used it both professionally and personally. I am a behavioral scientist trained in Jungian psychoanalysis and have had an active consulting practice focused on performance improvement of both the individual and the organization. Also, as an adjunct professor of behavioral science at Pepperdine University, I used THE CREEI PROCESS in my discussion as one way to analyze dreams. My students found the process both useful and interesting.

In my private practice working with individuals, I found THE CREEI PROCESS effective in helping the client get a better understanding of themselves and their behavioral style. This was significant in helping to improve their effectiveness. I use CREEI in organizational settings to get a quick look at the interaction pattern of the company's management team, dealing with each executive both individually and as part of the team. This allows a window into the effectiveness of the management team.

I also use THE CREEI PROCESS in my own company as a tool to increase performance. As an active consultant and CEO, I personally I use THE CREEI PROCESS to monitor my own behavior to stay balanced. The self-interview questions focused on any "no" or "don't know" answers allow me to become aware of where I'm personally out of balance and adjust my behavior appropriately. THE CREEI PROCESS has been an effective resource both personally and professionally. It is worth the effort to learn and utilize the process.

FATHER JOHN, RON HENNIES, D.MIN.
ORTHODOX CHURCH IN AMERICA

(Father John's doctorate is in liturgics, liturgical history and pastoral theology.)

For the last several years, I have been meeting with Eugene Kovalenko for discussions that range over matters from our past, the sharing of newly discovered books and almost unlimited subjects with the single exception of politics. One of the most persistent and fascinating matters of discussion has been that of our dreams. Eugene has developed a method of looking deeply into those dreams by means of a process that he calls THE CREEI PROCESS. Although I am not trained as a clinical

Jungian, I find this process helpful both personally and as a pastoral counselor.

In describing CREEI, perhaps it would be best to first say plainly what it is not. It is not some New Age substitute for traditional religious expression. It is no substitute for prayer, either corporate or private. It is no substitute for worship, again either corporate or private worship. Study of the religious scripture of both Christian and Jewish faiths enlivens and enriches the CREEI approach to dreams.

Christian scriptures contain more than 100 references to dreams and their effect upon the dreamer. Our exploration of our dreams puts us in good company. I have found the CREEI tool to be useful in my pastoral counseling, sometimes even profoundly useful. In the same way, I have found the CREEI method of looking at my own dreams to be both revealing and encouraging. Using this method does not depend upon some guru to offer us definition and enlightenment where our dreams are concerned. The tool may be used privately and may even be employed with another person without revealing the actual content of a dream.

We spend many hours in the state of sleep with attendant dreaming. Why should we ignore such a potential treasure trove? An adamant refusal to plumb the depths of our dreams may mean that we live only on the ego level of our lives and fail to listen to what may be a veritable gold mine of insight and of enlightenment. THE CREEI PROCESS is a most useful tool. I recommend its use on both a private and pastoral level.

KENDALL O. PRICE, PHD
LICENSED PSYCHOLOGIST IN CALIFORNIA AND LIFETIME
    MEMBER OF THE AMERICAN PSYCHOLOGICAL
    ASSOCIATION (Ken's last words to Eugene as he struggled
    to stay awake during Eugene's last visit, were: "You must
    publish CREEI! It is more important than you think.")

As a professionally-trained social psychologist with a 20+ year career as police psychologist for a major California city, I have found Dr. Kovalenko's CREEI Process of unique value. In my consulting practice, I have found that individuals are often wary of dream analysis. This is because they are usually thinking about a more traditional—and controversial—approach by Freud or Jung that deals with the meaning of dream symbols. When I show them THE CREEI PROCESS, which is more objective and even quantifiable, they are much more interested.

Since my retirement, I have been writing a book dealing with the skills and the character traits essential for personal effectiveness. The major part of the book is 2,000 quotations by 1,800 authors, but it also includes commentary based on my experiences in training, teaching and consulting. One major chapter deals with the importance of Knowing Yourself. For this chapter, I have asked Dr. Kovalenko to prepare a description of THE CREEI PROCESS, which will be invaluable to the reader in his personal journey to become more effective.

I believe the process is particularly useful in pastoral or confidential situations, since the questions can be asked and answered without ever disclosing personal images or material that would be embarrassing or inappropriate to share. However, this process can not only be applied personally but to groups in building morale or solving group problems. The questions can be asked of the group as an entity to assess the general state of balance of the group at large.

The main reason THE CREEI PROCESS is so well organized is because of Dr. Kovalenko's personal experience with his dreams. I know of few psychologists who have the 40 years of experience remembering and analyzing their own dreams as Dr. Kovalenko has done. He is truly an expert in this field.

Rex C. Mitchell, PhD
Professor of Management, California
State University, Northridge

As a management and organizational consultant for 38 years, I have found THE CREEI PROCESS to be useful in coaching a number of executive clients about work and life issues. As a psychotherapist, I used the process in helping individuals think about their dreams. As a university professor of management, I have found that the process can be a useful tool in teaching students how to manage their own lives and attitudes in developing their careers as potential managers and leaders. The process also has been helpful to me personally.

Karl Boyer

(This was an email that came unexpectedly one day in recent years as a pleasant surprise. Karl and I worked for the same engineering research company for several months in the late '70s. His note is evidence of our many conversations referring to how to put our dreams to work in practical ways on the job.)

Hello, this is a voice from the past, going back to E.C.P. days in El Segundo. We worked together on the Braton Cycle Turbine project. This is your assistant, Karl Boyer. It has been a very long time. I was thinking of you and how you enlightened me on using dreams to solve technical problems. I have never forgotten that, or you. Thank you so much...

The Rev. Dr. Gary Lee Baldwin
Priest in Charge (2013–2015), Trinity on the Hill
Episcopal Church, Los Alamos, New Mexico

Prior to my ordination into the priesthood of the Episcopal Church, I had been trained and served as a licensed psychotherapist. Part of my training was a significant introduction to Jungian dream work. I often found using this training quite helpful, especially when my work with clients encountered periods of impasse. Almost without exception, the therapeutic process became richly productive and healing.

This was also true in my vocational preparation to become a priest. I worked for a period of time with a Jungian therapist to better understand and grow in my spiritual maturity. Many sessions were spent in the rich exploration of my dream world.

Shortly after arriving at Trinity on the Hill Episcopal Church in Los Alamos, New Mexico, I was introduced to Dr. Eugene Kovalenko. I had been called to serve in this parish as their Priest in Charge during a time of intense transition following the 27-year service of their former clergy. My role was to assist the people of this parish through this transition by carefully looking at where they had been, where they were now and where God was leading them into the future. This was especially difficult as many of the parishioners were in various stages of grief. Eugene showed significant interest in my work. He suggested and offered to me the availability of a process he developed called CREEI. It was a process that allowed groups to explore their dreams in a group setting that promoted cohesion and growth.

At first, I was not sure as to how such a process would be accepted in this parish full of scientists. He then set up a special workshop to introduce me to the process for my evaluation. Skeptically, I attended. Sitting in the room were four or five other people I had just met or had only known a short time. After introducing the process to us, each of us was invited to share a dream. I found it somewhat intimidating sharing a dream, as it was like disclosing a very intimate aspect of me to what amounted to be strangers. Each of us, however, was, figuratively speaking, in the same boat. Shockingly, one person shared a dream he had the night before that was about me! In the dream, he described me as a father with six children. I was a bit stunned for I have no biological children. Later, in a private meeting with Eugene, the parts of this dream became more apparent, as I am a priest in a church denomination that refers to me as "father." I was presently serving in my sixth parish as a priest. In a sense then, I am the father of six children. Such information was not available to the conscious life of the dreamer. Further discussion revealed some other information that was significant about my current circumstances.

After a period of time I asked for volunteers within my parish to participate in THE CREEI PROCESS. We started out with twelve persons who came to the initial workshop. Four stayed on regularly for weekly meetings in which we put the process into action. What I found so very helpful was using a process that easily identified the types of dreams we shared, as well provided a tool to measure our changes and progress. It was interesting observing the changes in each of our dreams and lives over the period of the next several weeks. Mine went from TRAUMATIC dreams to TRANSFORMATIVE dreams. Part of this process was nurtured along with individual sessions of deeper dream exploration with Eugene. I became more aware of my personal spirituality strengthening, as my relationship with God deepened. My work as a priest in this intense setting became more effective. I also observed this in the lives of the others who were availing themselves of these sessions

THE CREEI PROCESS has been a strong addition to my understanding of dreams, as well as how this can be significantly applied in group settings. We who allowed ourselves to participate in this type of intimacy found our relationships becoming profoundly rich and unifying in the mysterious life of the Divine. I am a better priest and person because of it. Little did I know that when I first met Dr. Eugene Kovalenko how my life would be truly enriched and a profound new friendship began.

Victor Valenzuela
Chaplain for Post 8874 of the Veterans of Foreign Wars, Los Alamos, New Mexico

When I first heard about this process I was suspicious and told everybody that I didn't want any part of it. I did not want to be exposed to my past history about things I shouldn't talk about or were embarrassing. Fortunately, Eugene challenged me to attend a workshop before dismissing it out of hand.

I felt very blessed to take that initial step, because once I attended the first group meeting—it lasted about 2-1/2 hours—I was really excited. And I finished the subsequent six-week seminar. Once I got into it, it was extremely beneficial in terms of better understanding my inner self. Having recorded all the sessions, I review them every once in a while. And, I'm willing to continue the second phase to help new guys better understand how it works.

James Nesmith, Jr.
Vice Commander of Post 8874 of the Veterans of Foreign Wars, Los Alamos, New Mexico

Many of us who were in Vietnam have been through various sorts of treatments for lingering issues during that period. Most of them have not produced any significant results. This is a totally new approach to looking at the inner workings of the mind that is non-invasive and non-threatening and is a very effective means of opening those doors in the back recesses of the mind and bringing forth memories that seem to correlate with the dreams. I've found it to be very gratifying, helpful, insight-giving, and perception-building. It's been a big help.

Appendix F

Joseph Dillard has created a protocol called Integral Deep Listening (IDL) that takes individuals to greater understanding of a dream by taking them far beyond the original boundaries of the dream itself. He considers it a form of Dream Yoga, a discipline of awakening, lucidity, and movement toward enlightenment. IDL is ideal for dealing constructively with TRAUMATIC dreams that CREEI is not designed to handle. CREEI is only a door opener to appreciate the creative process, to experiencing the creative process, but IDL is a deeper, more powerful way to work with dreams if you are motivated to go deeper.

Here is an example of an IDL done by Eugene based on the dream Lucifer is Here! Which is presented in **APPENDIX G**. It was Eugene's first IDL interview and was done soon after Joseph Dillard first developed his IDL protocol. Notice the date of the dream was 1962 but the date of the IDL interview was 2006—a gap of 44 years! Despite this time gap, Eugene could revisit this dream via an IDL perspective and gain much new current information and wisdom.

The questions, placed in bold type, are the standard questions in Joseph Dillard's IDL protocol.[53]

IDL INTERVIEW: DECEMBER 3, 2006

JND (Joseph Dillard): What are three fundamental life issues that you are dealing with now in your life?

---

[53] We strongly encourage you to look at Joseph Dillard's on-line materials: https://www.dreamyoga.com

ENK (Eugene): 1. Being authentic. 2. Finding others who are or wish to be authentic. 3. Helping others be or become authentic.

JND: Tell a dream you remember....

ENK: "Lucifer is Here!"[54]

JND: Why do you think that you had this dream?

ENK: At the time of this dream, I was working as a graduate research assistant (GRA) to Dr. Birch Holt at the Lawrence Livermore National Laboratory in Livermore (LLNL), CA during the summer break from graduate school studies at the University of Utah. Before moving temporarily to Livermore for the summer, I had been called into the University of Utah Stake Mission presidency as counselor to Morris A. Kjar. I took this position seriously as a believing Mormon. The dream posits my relationship with two local Mormon priesthood holders, one my best friend, Cal, and the other the local Elders Quorum president. I was in a missionary mode of thinking, believing and behaving.

JND: If it were playing at a theater, what name would be on the marquee?

ENK: "Lucifer is here!"

JND: What are the characters in the dream?

ENK: Calvin, Monte, Meeting Room, Swirly Thing.

JND: If one character had something especially important to tell you, which would it be?

ENK: Swirly Thing (ST).

---

[54] For complete dream content, see **APPENDIX G.**

At this point Joseph Dillard asked Eugene (ENK) to engage in a dialogue with this dream character, Swirly Thing (ST), so Eugene was playing the part of both ENK and ST.

ENK: Swirly Thing, what do you think of my last interview with Joseph Smith Jr.?[55]

ST: It should be clear to you by now that all was not well in your experience with the local Mormon priesthood way back in 1962. I was trying to get your attention, since you were so obviously asleep. Instead, you became frightened and fought my attempts to alert you to the truth of that situation. Calvin symbolized your personal LDS male friendships. Monte symbolized your relationship to your local priesthood leadership.

ENK: I experienced you as an evil presence, trying to do me in.

ST: I came to alert you to an inauthentic communication from your colleague. I meant you no harm.

ENK: How does that apply to my last interview with Joseph Smith?

ST: It applies to your addiction to the Mormon priesthood that Joseph established. It is not as it claims to be and your colleague did not speak the truth. He was not being authentic and you did not know how to honor or interpret your own intense and authentic feelings about what he was saying. I was trying to communicate with you, but you were not conscious enough to hear or understand me.

ENK: Well, my friend Joseph Dillard asks me to have you score on the six categories that he presents for evaluating interviews. They are: How would you score yourself, 0 to 10, in

---

[55] See: Dialogues with Joseph, Part 1. Annealing and Healing, Appendix, 2006 Salt Lake City Sunstone Symposium.

confidence, compassion, wisdom, acceptance, peace of mind and witnessing? Will you do that please?

ST: Happy to oblige. Ten in all categories.

ENK: Wow! Boy, did I misunderstand you.

ST: You did indeed!

At this point Joseph Dillard (JND) took over the questioning of Swirly Thing.

JND: Swirly Thing, would you please tell me what you look like and what you are doing?

ST: I am a whirlwind and have come to warn and rescue Eugene.

JND: What do you like most about yourself in this experience? What are your strengths?

ST: I am powerful and focused on my mission to warn and rescue Eugene.

JND: What do you dislike most about yourself? Do you have weaknesses? What?

ST: I do not dislike myself and have no weaknesses. I am able to accomplish what I have been assigned to do.

JND: If you could change this dream in any way you wanted, would you?

ST: No.

JND: If that dream were to continue, what would happen next?

ST: The dream accomplished its purpose in warning Eugene. He did not appear to understand the warning at the time. Eugene will eventually wake up to the more general dangers he is encountering.

JND: Swirly Thing, if you could be anywhere you wanted to be and take any form you desired, would you change? If so, how?

ST: There is no other form I can conceive of better designed to get Eugene to reflect on the relationships he is making.

JND: Swirly Thing, what aspect of Eugene do you represent or most closely personify?

ST: Spiritual power.

JND: Swirly Thing, how would you score yourself 0 to 10, in confidence, compassion, wisdom, acceptance, peace of mind and witnessing?

ST: Tens in all categories.

JND: Swirly Thing, how would Eugene's life be different if he naturally scored high in all six of these qualities all the time?

ST: Greatly different. At the time of the dream, he scores 5, 4, 3, 3, 2 and 2 respectively. God only knows how his life would be different if he scored all 10s. Clearly, he has lots of awakening to do! But he still has to suffer the consequences of his unconsciousness.

JND: Swirly Thing, if you could live Eugene's waking life for him, how would you live it differently?

ST: It is not for me to live Eugene's waking life. He is due for some rude awakenings over the next five years.

JND: Swirly Thing, if you could live Eugene's waking life for him today, would you handle his three life issues differently? If so, how?

ST: These are good life issues now. He has had a difficult time coming up with them.

JND: Swirly Thing, what three life issues would you focus on if you were in charge of his life?

ST: Those listed might be more clearly identified with the six Dream Yoga quality scoring metrics.

JND: Swirly Thing, in what life situations would it be most beneficial for Eugene to imagine that he is you and act as you would?

ST: When confronted by overconfidence, he should get to know, understand and trust me. I am not the devil.

JND: Swirly Thing, why do you think that you are in this dream?

ST: To awaken Eugene to his inflation and overconfidence.

JND: Eugene, what have you heard yourself say?

ENK: I am asleep and need to awaken to reality. My relationships with male friends and Mormon priesthood holders are not as authentic as I believed they are.

JND: If this experience were a wake-up call from your soul, what do you think it would be saying to you?

ENK: Be alert to the truth of your feelings.

Note 1: Long after this IDL protocol version was used by ENK, Joseph Dillard updated it to ask a further general question with respect to quantifying the six qualities, namely, "Why that quantity?"

Note 2: In terms of the "anticipatory" aspect of this earliest (1962) ANTICIPATORY-TRAUMATIC *dream, ENK learned many years later what happened in the outer world to one of his dream characters 'Cal,' who eventually left the Mormon Church and became a Protestant* minister. As for Monte, ENK lost track of him completely and only later heard distressing rumors about what may have happened to him. In any case, there was a seeming confirmation of what "Swirly Thing" had warned powerfully about in the dream. That is, things were not as they seemed at the time.

Here is a later IDL that Eugene did with Joseph Dillard that includes the question "why." It is presented primarily to give a taste of the profound extension of the dream experience by IDL. Insights that the interviewee receives in this hypnosis-like experience go far beyond the insights from THE CREEI PROCESS.

IDL INTERVIEW: APRIL 13, 2011

JND: What are three fundamental life issues that you are dealing with now in your life?

ENK: 1. Getting the Los Alamos Deep Democracy Open Forum (LADDOF) enterprise financially stable; 2. Following up on the Denver 2011 symposium contacts; 3. Exploring military applications of CREEI and IDL.

JND: Tell me a dream you remember.

ENK:

I am with Joseph Dillard. Earlier he has been making a dream-work training presentation to a military unit. I have headphones on and have telephoned the unit for information on how the presentation is received. A woman answers phone with a standard greeting identifying the unit. Then I hear a male voice of a senior military officer announcing how effective dream work can be in military applications.

I have come to pick Joseph up in a Jeep-like vehicle at the military unit's building. We take off from the building into a rough, winding hilly dirt road that soon becomes muddy. Joseph begins to shout, "Jesus H. Christ, Eugene! This isn't going to get us anywhere!", I say, "Not to worry. That's the beauty of these four-wheel-drive all-terrain vehicles." Just as it looks like we are coming

*to a cul-de-sac on an upgrade, we come upon an easily-
accessed, level, paved residential area.*

JND: Why do you think that you had this dream?

ENK: I think it had to do with meeting the most surprising contact
at a Denver symposium administered by Arnold Mindell
and his Process Work team. The contact is a young Major
Joar A. H. of the Philippine Military Academy's Education,
Plans and Programs department and a seven-year combat
veteran. He prides himself on the accuracy of his intuitive
combat decisions and is interested in my military background,
especially ideas about parapsychological warfare defense
preparedness. He is heading for Fort Bragg, S.C., to attend a
four-month training on parapsychological warfare.

JND: If it were playing at a theater, what name would be on
the marquee?

ENK: Parapsychological Warfare Defense Preparedness.

JND: What are the characters in the dream?

ENK: The characters are: Joseph Dillard, Jeep-like vehicle, building,
rugged dirt and mud terrain, earphones, woman on line,
senior military officer, cul-de-sac, level residential area.

JND: If a character had something especially important to tell you,
which would it be?

ENK: Jeep.

JND: Now I want to address questions to only that dream character
for a little while. Jeep, would you please tell me what you look
like and what you are doing?

ENK now answers as the character of the Jeep.

Jeep: I am a small, U.S. Army-like issue of a military all-terrain vehicle and am at the service of Eugene as he maneuvers in his perception of his spiritual work, i.e., his "job."

JND: Jeep, what do you like most about yourself in this dream? What are your strengths?

Jeep: I am sturdy, dependable and fast.

JND: Jeep, what do you dislike most about yourself? Do you have weaknesses? What?

Jeep: Nothing to dislike; no weaknesses.

JND: Jeep, if you could change this experience in any way you wanted, would you? If so, how would you change it?

Jeep: No.

JND: Jeep, if that experience were to continue, what would happen next?

Jeep: Eugene would follow up on his contact with Major Joar and then he and Joseph would collaborate on developing military applications as an extension of the presentation that Joseph delivered earlier in the dream.

JND: Jeep, if you could be anywhere you wanted to be and take any form you desired, would you change? If so, how?

Jeep: No.

JND: Jeep, you are in Eugene's dream, correct? He created you, right?

Jeep: Yes.

JND: Jeep, what aspect of Eugene do you represent or most closely personify?

Jeep: His military awareness and flexibility.

JND: Jeep, if you could live Eugene's waking life for him, how would you live it differently?

Jeep: I wouldn't. It's fascinating to watch it evolve as the spirit leads....

JND: Jeep, if you could live Eugene's waking life for him today, would you handle his three life issues differently? If so, how?

Jeep: No.

JND: Jeep, what three life issues would you focus on if you were in charge of his life?

Jeep: I cannot answer.

JND: Jeep, how would you score yourself 0 to 10 in confidence, compassion, wisdom, acceptance, peace of mind and witnessing? And why?

Jeep:

> *Confidence:* Ten. I do what I am designed to do with no fear of failing.
>
> *Compassion:* Zero. I do whatever Eugene directs, but without feeling. That is his business.
>
> *Wisdom:* Zero. I do whatever Eugene directs, but without judgment. That is his business.
>
> *Acceptance:* Ten. I do whatever Eugene directs;
>
> *Peace of Mind:* Ten. I am at peace with whatever Eugene directs;
>
> *Witnessing:* Ten. I can see the big picture as it unfolds in Eugene's story

JND: Jeep, if you scored tens in all six of these qualities, would you be different? If so, how?

Jeep: Yes, I would be more like a horse.

JND: Jeep, how would Eugene's life be different if he naturally scored high in all six of these qualities all the time?

Jeep: He is close to these qualities some of the time, but his life would probably not be much different from what it is now.

JND: Jeep, in what life situations would it be most beneficial for Eugene to imagine that he is you and act as you would?

Jeep: I do not believe it would be beneficial for Eugene not to have compassion or wisdom. I follow his directions without concern for being compassionate or wise.

JND: Jeep, why do you think that you are in this dream?

Jeep: To give Eugene yet another vehicular option in navigating his life's journey and to remind him that his military life is not yet over.

JND: Eugene, what have you heard yourself say?

ENK: I am still concerned with the parapsychological warfare defense issues that took me to visit J.B. Rhine at Duke University in November 1964. They are even more important these days.

JND: If this experience were a wake-up call from your soul, what do you think it would be saying to you?

ENK: Be alert for opportunities to teach spiritual warfare defense applications using my own and Joseph Dillard's dream work techniques, as well as those of Arnold Mindell.

Appendix G

THE CREEI PROCESS has had a gradual evolution to its present form. It was entirely the creation of the first author, Eugene Kovalenko, who wanted to develop a tool for understanding dreams that was simple, direct, self-evident and immediately applicable. Especially interesting is the observation that the process evolved largely through Eugene's key personal dreams together with those of others with whom he could share this subject. The process is about dreams and came from dreams. Here is how THE CREEI PROCESS was developed by Eugene Kovalenko, as he tells it.

FIRST REMEMBERED AND RECORDED DREAM: A NIGHTMARE

During graduate school in 1962 at the University of Utah, I had a nightmare that profoundly affected me. It was my first remembered dream, which I wrote down. At the time, I was in a leadership position in an extracurricular assignment in the Mormon tradition in which I had been raised. The nightmare was a wakeup call to a new reality and shook my commitment to my mission assignment. And it launched in me a new attitude in my overall search for truth. I called the nightmare "Lucifer is here!"

Eugene

LUCIFER IS HERE!, 1962

I'm in conversation with old friend Cal[56] and new friend Monte.[57] Monte says, "I feel that I have acquired new understanding. Things are fine, all is well." Suddenly a dark tingling sensation comes over me and the thought flashes into my mind to shout: "Look out, brethren! Lucifer is here!" But, before I can utter a sound, I am bound by some black essence and feel myself starting to be dragged down and away into some mysterious, nebulous waste. I look at Cal and try to gain his attention so that he can cast this terrible influence from me, but he pays no attention and continues to talk to Monte. In terror, I try to scream his name, but cannot produce even a groan. Instead, the blackness engulfs me and I feel myself swirling around and around and down, the vision of my friends fading from view. Several times this swirling, engulfing blackness reoccurs, but never the view of my friends again.

CREEI SCORE: . . . . . **+?+−−//?−−//?+??**
ANTICIPATORY-TRAUMATIC

I learned that dreams, especially nightmares like this one, can have profound and long-lasting effects on my memory. I didn't know what to do with them yet.

---

[56] Cal: physicist and personal best friend at Lawrence Livermore National Laboratory.
[57] LDS ward elders quorum president.

REMEMBERING MY DREAMS

It was not until late October, 1964, after reading Hugh Lynn Cayce's newly published book, Venture Inward,[58] that I learned quickly how to recall my dreams. In fact, that very night I began inviting, remembering and recording my dreams. From then on, I began to keep a dream journal,[59] which has become a continuing source of insight and understanding when later reviewed and reprocessed. Even today my old dreams continue to take on new meaning.

LISTENING TO DREAMS AS DEFENSE AGAINST PSYCHIC WARFARE

As I became more and more aware of my dreams I reflected on various experiences I have had. One was the experience of being involved with a top secret military operation when I was in the U.S. Army. That CIA-MI6 joint venture in 1954 involved tunneling from the American sector of West Berlin into the Soviet sector of East Berlin and tapping both German and Soviet Red Army telephone lines for KGB intelligence.[60]

I was recruited from the staff of the Russian Department at the Army Language School because of my skills in Russian translation and, ironically, my role as the leading bass singer for the popular Army Language School Russian Choir made up of American soldiers. While stationed in Berlin I became aware of unusual and troubling insights that eventually made me aware of parapsychological phenomena years

---

[58] Cayce, Hugh Lynn.

[59] For much more detail about Eugene's dreams check his personal blogs: https://creeiprocess.blogspot.com/ and https://orthodoxodyssey.blogspot.com

[60] Long time classified, this has now been declassified and I can finally talk about it. The fascinating story is detailed in two print documentary editions (2002 and 2013) by Professor David Stafford titled "Spies Beneath Berlin", a British film documentary with the same title (now on YouTube), and the most recent print documentary (2019) by journalist Steve Vogel titled "Betrayal in Berlin." Not being allowed to talk about this for 20 years caused this author considerable emotional turmoil.

later after taking a PhD in engineering science in late spring 1964. I began to search the literature, as any good scientist would do, only to discover an array of information that seemed irresponsible, chaotic or fanciful.

In November 1964 I had the privilege to meet with Professor J.B. Rhine at Duke University who was widely regarded as "The Father of Parapsychology." When I explained the origin of my postwar concern to him he immediately encouraged me to join him to pursue the issue of parapsychological warfare defense. Most people are very resistant to acknowledging the very existence of parapsychological phenomena and I was anxious to figure out a way of working around that resistance, including my own.

Shortly after my meeting with Rhine, during our initial negotiation of how to proceed with the psiwarfare defense project, I had a pivotal dream which seemed a "red herring" kind of dream at the time, apparently having nothing to do with our mutual concern. That dream has only recently become clear to me in that it had very much to do with what was shortly to come to pass in my future relationship to Rhine, as well as to my then job and personal life.

Eugene

FUGITIVE WOMAN, December 23, 1964

Scene 1. Hiding under a house.

*I am a beautiful woman with a bad
reputation. Always being taken advantage of (no
specific instance that I can remember) but am
a kind of fugitive. Some wives are jealous; some
hypocrite husbands would have me put away. I run.
Hide. Sleep under a house. They pass me by.*

CREEI SCORE: . . . . . **+?+--//-+-//?+??**

ANTICIPATORY-TRAUMATIC

Scene 2. At the Temple.

I am still the beautiful woman and return
to my locker (in the temple) to get my things.
Can't find my briefcase. A conference of seminary
administrators is meeting. They look wholesome.
They do not notice me though my locker is nearby.
I am in Levis and T-shirt, mussed up from having
struggled the day before and slept under the house.
A woman friend with locker next to mine tells me:
"[so and so] is not going to say anything when you
tell your side of the story. She's just going to remain
silent and pretend she doesn't know what you're
talking about."

CREEI SCORE: . . . . . **+++−?//−++//++?+**

ANTICIPATORY

That I had this dream on the birthday of Joseph Smith, founder of Mormonism, seemed significant. Later I thought it was about my relationship to the Mormon Church in which I was raised, but from which I became ex-communicated shortly thereafter. From my perspective now I see that it had everything to do with the threat of deliberate as well as unconsciously intentional parapsychological warfare that we live under in this country, and that my subsequent work at developing THE CREEI PROCESS stemmed from a goal to find a way that the domination of thinking over feeling could be overcome. CREEI bypasses that domination, and this dream helped me to understand that.[61]

---

[61] https://orthodoxodyssey.blogspot.com/2009/01/23-dec-64-dream-from-todays-perspective.html

JUNGIAN ANALYSIS

Over a year later in 1966, having gone through major life changes of job, marriage and church membership, I met my wife-to-be Lawrene, who was training to become a Jungian analyst. She introduced me to Jungian psychology and made it possible to enter Jungian analysis with a well-known Beverly Hills psychiatrist. This led me to a deeper appreciation for dreams, which I faithfully continued to record.

Another example of old dreams examined is a dream Eugene had in early 1966, after committing to enter Jungian analysis.

> ### Eugene
> GREAT CHAIN, March 1966
>> Scene 1. Dark Clouds.
>> *I am witnessing a vast panorama—great dark clouds over a wide desert scene. In the far distance, I see a great chain coming out of the clouds and into the earth below. In the foreground, I see a small boy holding onto a chord or rope that is going into the clouds above. He does not know what he is holding onto, and he also knows his mother does not believe him. In the area below between the rope into the sky and the chain coming down into the ground, I see a structure of two white mobile or manufactured homes at right angles to each other.*
>
>> CREEI SCORE: . . . . . **+-+--//???//++??**
>> ANTICIPATORY-TRAUMATIC

Scene 2. Invitation.

I am in the nearest white mobile home with Lawrene. I ask her to look out at the great chain and the desert drama. She does not seem impressed as I am. Instead she takes me by the hand into the bedroom, as we are naked but wrapped in white towels.

CREEI SCORE: . . . . . **+++++//?++//?+++**

MOTIVATIONAL

Scene 3. Wrong Room.

I am in the other white mobile home with two young women who are my students. I am showing them the great chain drama, which intrigues them. But then I notice that the room we are in is the men's room and gently urge us to find a more appropriate place to continue our discussion.

CREEI SCORE: . . . . . **+++++//+++//++++**

TRANSFORMATIVE

My dream "GREAT CHAIN" contained three scenes.
The painting captures only the first scene ('Dark Clouds'),
which scored ANTICIPATORY-TRAUMATIC.

I had this dream before CREEI scoring was developed, but have forgotten why I scored only the first scene. When I revisited the dream many years later for this book in 2017, I was surprised and delighted to to discover that the second and third scenes scored MOTIVATIONAL and TRANSFORMATIVE, respectively. The delay in scoring revealed how new, meaningful insights can be found in a more careful review of an important old dream. In this case it begins dark and threatening, but leads to a MOTIVATIONAL bridge with a TRANSFORMATIVE ending!

PRACTICAL RESULTS FROM LISTENING TO DREAMS

For a while, I did not do much more than record my dreams, but in 1975, I had an experience that taught me about the direct and useful connection between a dream and outer events. I had been hired by a firm that made thermocouples to be used in nuclear power reactors. The company was having a terrible quality control problem with contamination of certain devices, specifically zirconium-coated thermocouples. After lengthy interviews over the course of six or seven weeks with all employees and careful examination of every step in the manufacturing process of the thermocouples, the search narrowed to the unsuspected certified cleaning agent itself, a certain kind of alcohol. That turned out to be the problem! What was trusted wasn't to be trusted. For some reason, I went back to my dream journal and discovered a dream that I'd had on the first night of the interviews. I saw a phrase in the dream with the words "contaminated alcohol." Had I been more alert to this potential connection at the time, it would have been the clue that would have saved the company much time and effort and money, but it taught me that dreams can convey practical and meaningful information.

A DREAM CAN PROFOUNDLY CHANGE YOU

On my birthday, November 17, 1975, I had a two-part dream that had a surprising impact on me, which made me realize how TRANSFORMATIVE dreams can be. Until this dream, I had had only negative interactions with African-Americans, both through my upbringing in the LDS church and in the US Army.

Eugene
ENCOUNTERING BLACKS,[62] November 17, 1975

Scene 1. Hand Grab

I am a passenger with Diane[63] in her car, a VW beetle (which corresponds to her car in reality). I see another vehicle, a pickup truck, coming from the opposite direction carrying a group of young black men. I have my left arm hanging out the window and as we pass, one of them grabs my hand. The hand grasp is almost too much for me, but I tell Diane to keep driving so as not to get off course. The black youth finally lets go.

CREEI SCORE: . . . . . **+++++//+--//++?+**

TRAUMATIC

Scene 2. Black Boy Grabs Leg

I am in a men's locker room. A small black boy comes up to me, silently grabs hold of my right leg and holds on. I am shocked, indignant and try to peel him off with the heel of my right hand pushing on his head. But I can't get him off because he is surprisingly strong and so tenacious that there seems no way I am going to get this kid off of me. And then I realize, wait a minute! What am I doing? This is a child! He's not attacking me! All he wants is a connection; all he wants is to be held. Suddenly, understanding and compassion sweep through me

---

[62] At the time of this dream, Mormon doctrine towards African-Americans was officially racist. Until June 8, 1978 they used the word "negro" and that is why Eugene used this term in his dream journal. As an active Mormon at the time, Eugene had taken a strong objection to this doctrine in earlier years and had been punished for it. Nevertheless, he was apparently still suffering from its inner repercussions until this dream showed him a deeper, transformative truth.

[63] Eugene's real life friend and colleague.

and I reach down to pick the boy up. That is all he wants—to be embraced, uplifted and held. He does not speak, but is now beaming and smiling, cradled in my arms.

CREEI SCORE: . . . . . **+++++//+++//++++**

TRANSFORMATIVE

That was a revelation! This birthday dream suddenly changed my whole inner racial prejudicial structure.

Then, what happened that very afternoon in outer life was totally unexpected. I was introduced to the second black man I'd ever met, a black minister friend of Diane's, whom she wanted me to sing for. My TRANSFORMATIVE dream that morning allowed me to meet and relate to this man without residual prejudice. After singing extemporaneously for him, he immediately hired me to sing Negro Spirituals for his Sunday morning radio broadcasts from his church in the Watts district of south central Los Angeles.

In January 1976, I had a dream that inspired me to be aware of a calling that was to make a major difference in my life.

Eugene
DREAM CALL TO A "GRACE-FILLED MINISTRY",
January 1976

I wake up hearing a clear, commanding masculine voice saying:

"It is time to wake up and begin a grace-filled ministry!"

I thought: who is speaking and what does it mean? It was saying "Wake up! Wake up! Wake up!"

CREEI SCORE: . . . . . **+?+--//?++//++?+**

ANTICIPATORY

It was not clear what the "ministry" was to be, but it was literally a wake-up call, which put me into an anticipatory attitude. It occurs to me only now at the time of this writing that this dream date, 1976, is not only anticipating my subsequent UCLA course later that year, but the date I could finally publicly disclose my classified military experience, which would be June 1976. I had been forbidden to speak about it for twenty years after being separated from the US Army in April 1956.

COURSE AT UCLA

Soon after the January 1976 dream, a long-time Mormon friend who was an administrator at UCLA invited me to teach a course.[64]

Because of my recent dream, I decided to develop an experimental course called "Creative Dreaming and Spiritual Awakening." A book by Patricia Garfield[65] greatly influenced this course. A small group at Bel Air Presbyterian Church helped me to develop the curriculum for this course, which enjoyed moderate success for two quarters. This experience taught me that dreams were an appropriate subject for academic study.

CENTER FOR FEELING THERAPY

During the ten years after the 1976 UCLA course, I continued to be interested in dreams. In 1986, while employed for several years by an aerospace engineering firm, I became aware of an organization called the Center for Feeling Therapy located in Los Angeles. It was headed by two young psychologists, Richard Corriere and Joseph Hart. Their work is described in their book, The Dream Makers.[66] The best lesson that I learned from them was the value of objectively talking about the structure of dreams in contrast to their content. It taught me that

---

[64] UCLA Dream Course, Los Angeles Times, September 9, 1976
[65] *Creating Dreaming*, Garfield, Patricia.
[66] Corriere, Richard and Joseph Hart

dreams could be looked at objectively, whereas before I had considered them only subjectively, as in Freudian and Jungian analysis approaches.

DREAMS CAN REVEAL GROUP PROBLEMS
– A DREAM WORKSHOP

At about the same time, I had an experience at the aerospace engineering firm that taught me how sharing dreams can have a powerful and effective impact on group interactions. The company in general, including the engineering department I managed, was experiencing a serious morale problem. The general manager let me know that I needed to do something quickly to turn my group around.

I began to study this problem by bringing in each employee individually for an interview to get to know them more personally even though I had known them for several years. My individual interviews included risking a casual suggestion at the end of each interview. Something like "Oh, and by the way, if you should have a dream about anything to do with work, I would be most interested to know."

The very next morning, Betty, one of my engineering staff, whom I had known for more than five years, shared a dream she had the very next morning.[67] She dreamed that one of the engineers in our department was undergoing great distress and was concerned about him. This was risky because I was not sure if it was the engineer who was in distress or the dreamer herself who was in distress. Because we knew each other well, I asked if she would share her dream with that engineer.

It turned out that her perception of the engineer was accurate, which allowed me to understand and rectify the problem that was confronting him. (The engineer was a foreign national, whose English language skills were challenged. He had been losing sleep and weight and was greatly suffering about something he had not been able to discuss

------

[67] This is the dream that set the scene, which led to THE CREEI PROCESS. It illustrates an example of incubating a dream. But I intuited that it warranted taking the significant risk of her sharing her dream of the engineer in her dream with the engineer, himself. It could have had embarrassing, if not disastrous consequences. Providentially, it opened the door to engaging the company to a new way of communicating and solving morale problems.

with anyone in the company.) The resulting understanding among him and others in the department allowed me to adjust job descriptions, which significantly improved departmental morale and the way people in the group interacted. The culture of the group became one of mutual care as a consequence of the shared dream.

When the general manager saw this change, he asked me to apply what we were doing in my department to the whole company. This developed into a series of weekly two-hour sessions for the managers of all departments on a volunteer basis in which people were invited to share their dreams. THE CREEI PROCESS had not yet been developed.

One of the results of these weekly sessions allowed me to solve a personal problem I had with the general manager, whom I experienced as being controlling and domineering. However, a dream that this manager shared with me immediately after one of the weekly sessions changed how I perceived him. Overnight, I felt the misperceived burden of distrust evaporate! It was I who changed.

General Manager
SHIP'S CAPTAIN, 1987
I am a ship's captain and have a lot of responsibility for the safety of the ship and the crew. As a result, I know I must maintain a tight ship and crew.

CREEI SCORE: . . . . . **+++++//??+//++??**

TRAUMATIC

I realized at once that I had misjudged this man. He was truly concerned about his company, having a "tight ship," and really wasn't a tyrant at all, but a dedicated ship's captain. That was how he saw himself, and that allowed me to see him in a completely different light. It changed my attitude immediately. Then, after about six weeks of weekly two-hour sessions, one of the participants, my secretary, Linda, shared this ultimately transforming dream with the group.

Linda

MANAGERS FIGHTING, 1987

*Two managers [Gary and Lou] are falling
out of the clouds on parachutes, banging into and
bloodying each other and fighting on their way
down, until they are onto the ground. One of them,
the production control manager, has a white towel,
which he throws in and walks away.*

CREEI SCORE: . . . . . **+-+--//--?//????**
ANTICIPATORY-TRAUMATIC

The imagery was so compelling that it was immediately clear to the group that the conflict between these two departmental managers, who of all managers should have been working closely together, was what was causing the morale problem in the whole company. All employees had seen it, but didn't feel free to talk about it. Despite this fear, these two men now saw it for themselves and it became crystal clear that this was where the problem was! Those two and everyone else in attendance broke out laughing and the ice of the morale problem was broken. And, because they became aware of their previously out-of-awareness conflict, they were now able to work it out between themselves. Their willingness to acknowledge what they had been unable to acknowledge earlier resolved the root cause of the conflict and turned the company around immediately as the morale of the company soon went up. The problem was solved through THE CREEI PROCESS of sharing dreams, an instructive example of the power of dreams when brought to awareness.

CROFEC EVOLVES TO CREEI

Early in 1987, shortly after having been promoted to engineering manager at the aerospace company, I had an insight in which I recognized how the principles regarding the structure of dreams that I had learned from the Center for Feeling Therapy could be applied to my work situation. I initially called my insight CROFEC, an acronym for clarity, role, feeling, expression and contact. I then developed the idea of grading each answer to the dream questions on a 0 to 10 basis, realizing from my engineering background that these numbers could be used to track how a person's dreams evolve through time.

Later that year, I realized that more was needed, so I added ten more parameters, the first five of which (clarity, role, emotion, expression and intimacy) gave birth to the acronym CREEI. To the original five parameters, a sixth was added: completion. Then in 1991 at the suggestion of friend and former wife, Lawrene, the second set of questions were added, which then totaled fifteen.

CROSS-CULTURAL APPLICATION

In 1988, I conducted a CREEI presentation in Kiev, Ukraine, prior to the breakup of the Soviet Union. I wanted to see if this process would translate to other cultures. I was pleased to find that it worked with a group of Soviet psychologists, psychiatrists and social workers, all of whom at that time were obliged to be externally governed by Marxist ideology. The process demonstrated itself to be nonpolitical and nonsectarian and, thus, appropriate for virtually any audience.

THE CREEI INSTITUTE

In 1990, I developed an institute in Ventura, California, called the CREEI Institute. It started to grow quickly and proved successful in helping participants resolve personal and group problems. However, for unforeseen reasons, the institute did not evolve as planned and has not been operational since 1992.

CREEI PATTERNS EMERGE

In 1991 I held a CREEI Institute workshop and seminar in Ventura for an engineering group based in nearby Santa Paula,

California. That is the group that included Raul and Paula described at the end of Chapter 4. One of the participants asked if I had ever scored the dreams of the Bible. I thought that was a great question and directly went home that night to score those that I could find, and observing that most of them were prophetic dreams. I also realized that most of them fell into similar patterns even much like dreams of my own that I remembered. I had not thought before about trying to group dreams together into similar patterns. I did not want to call them prophetic or precognitive, but since they all seemed to be anticipating events in the future I dubbed them "ANTICIPATORY." I also realized that many of my dreams with similar patterns had triggered subsequent déjà vu experiences.

These Biblical dreams were so strikingly similar that I wondered if other dreams could have similar patterns. The next obvious recognizable pattern was when all of the questions were answered (+). These dreams triggered for me a feeling of joyful transformation and so I named them TRANSFORMATIVE. Next were the dreams that were only one or two questions short of TRANSFORMATIVE, motivating me to see how they could have been TRANSFORMATIVE. So they were "MOTIVATIONAL." Finally when many of the (−)'s were in the second set of six questions I felt a bit traumatized by them, and so they were called "TRAUMATIC." These patterns have proven useful in understanding the meaning of my own dreams.

QUICK APPLICATION OF CREEI IN A GROUP WITHOUT GETTING INTO CONTENT

Here is the story of one of the first times I used the simplified CREEI Process on a consulting assignment. It is also a great example of what THE CREEI PROCESS can accomplish for a group.

In early 1991, after creating the CREEI Institute, I was invited to conduct a workshop on THE CREEI PROCESS for the board of directors of a national educational institution based in Aspen, Colorado that was meeting for their annual review in a secluded place in Sedona,

Arizona. This was where the idea originated to do it quickly in a group without getting into content. One of the members of the board had been through my process a year or so previously and wanted me to come and present it to the other seventeen board members, who were meeting to discuss strategy and finances. I thought I had been invited to present a whole day's workshop, but then sat in that board room for six or seven hours while they went about their business. Instead of being introduced and beginning a workshop, no one even looked at me during that time and I began wondering why I was even there.

Finally, with only half an hour left until adjournment, the chairman looked at me and said, "Now, Dr. Kovalenko, you have 20 minutes to give us an image." Startled at first, I immediately asked them all to just remember a dream or an event. We went through the process of asking the 12 questions quickly and collectively while I wrote on a chalk board and after the scores evolved, I looked at the patterns that emerged and realized at once they had a major problem.

I said, "Folks, it is clear to me that you are here to make important decisions. Unfortunately, you are not going to make those decisions with any wisdom unless you deal with what seems to me to be anger or fear appearing in your dreams. I am seeing in your dream scores high levels of negative emotions. And without recognizing and resolving those negative scores, I don't see how you can make any of the decisions you are called upon to make, unless you first deal among yourselves with those conflicts."

As intelligent, serious educators, they understood at once, accepted my observation and immediately changed their agenda to focus on dealing with the kinds of things with which they were conflicted. The group had important but unexpressed inner emotions that created fear and anger. They realized the need to deal with those promptly and I felt I had done my job.

MOVE TO NEW MEXICO

I moved to Santa Fe, New Mexico, in spring 1992 and eventually took a consulting job at the Los Alamos National Laboratory in spring 1993.

During that first year in Santa Fe I conducted several workshops for the community and attended the 1993 annual conference of the International Association for the Study of Dreams (IASD), which had chosen Santa Fe that year. That's when I met Eric Craig, one of IASD's past presidents, who took a strong interest in CREEI. After working with him a while, he urged me to reduce the 15 questions to the current 12 as being more practical. I agreed.

It also had became apparent before moving to New Mexico that the 0 to 10 scoring in answering the CREEI questions was too burdensome. This observation was made by psychiatrist friend, Alan Bains, who was interested in investing in the CREEI Institute. I then simplified the answers to the present three options: yes (+), no (−) or uncertain (?).

In 2006, I became familiar with the profound work of Ken Wilber after reading his popular book, *A Brief History of Everything*. This helped me to apply with confidence THE CREEI PROCESS to many more groups since. I recognized that dreams are a way for the macrocosm within us to communicate with the microcosm outside of us, both presented in Ken Wilber's work. Here is the dream I had immediately after reading Wilber's book.

Eugene
MACROCOSM WITHIN, OCTOBER 5, 2006
*I am with some people to whom I am
passionately expressing my appreciation for the
12th-century Sufi poet Rumi's revelation that the
microcosm is that which is external to us and that*

the macrocosm is that which is within each of us individually.

CREEI SCORE: . . . . . **+++++//+++//++++**

TRANSFORMATIVE

THE CREEI PROCESS has proven to be a valid mechanism for developing integrity that would challenge the egotism that is so rampant in our society. The process taps into our out-of-awareness self and respects it, bypassing the ego and allowing the out-of-awareness self to express itself. These experiences demonstrate the idea of using dreams in a wide variety of situations, including business, church, school and community groups.

Thinking that we had come to the end of our manuscript text, Bob and I were surprised by an email from Rex Mitchell, one of my closest friends, who has followed the development of CREEI from its inception in 1987. We had sent Rex the latest draft for his inspection and he responded with the following email:

Rex Mitchell

CREEI DREAM ELEMENTS, July 31, 2020

In the evening of July 31, 2020, as I was starting my sleep for the night, I had a lucid dream: no people, no movement — just a completely-formed image representing the CREEI twelve questions. There were five spheres floating in space against a sky background, arranged in a line from my left to right, colored a shiny royal blue (the five CREEI). Below them, on the ground, were seven square tiles, arranged in two rows, three then four farther from me; they were a shiny rich tan color. The image was very clear, bright, and pleasant.

CREEI SCORE: . . . . . **++???//?++//+++**+

ANTICIPATORY

Rex's dream seems a fitting, remarkable, current end to the manuscript.

BOB'S WELCOME CONTRIBUTION

This book would not be possible without co-author Bob Thomsen's invaluable participation. In late 2007, I conducted a CREEI workshop in Los Alamos, New Mexico, which was attended by local residents including Bob and others from surrounding states. Because of his initial experience, we struck up an after-workshop acquaintance, which has blossomed into a close friendship. In recent years we would meet weekly at a local coffee shop where we would discuss far ranging ideas including a radical array of topics far beyond ordinary discussions.

In 2014 my health began to decline. I began to see my life slipping away and was in despair that my legacy involving CREEI would evaporate with me. At coffee one day "in a moment of weakness" Bob offered to help write a book about it, and so we embarked on this project together with no idea it would take so many years to complete.

In the course of writing this book together Bob has added many ideas of his own, especially relating to the application of THE CREEI PROCESS to non-dream situations, which has stretched the scope of the book far beyond its original vision. In particular, he included examining the dreams of pioneering psychiatrists Sigmund Freud, Carl Jung and legendary Russian author Leo Tolstoy, as well as conducted several IDL personal interviews with me using Joseph Dillard's remarkable protocols.

I cannot thank him enough for his commitment, friendship, imagination, care and wisdom. A more valuable friend I cannot imagine.

References

Alexander, Eben. Proof of Heaven: A Neurosurgeon's Journey into the Afterlife. New York: Simon & Schuster Paperbacks, 2012.

Bayliss, Jan. Aids to Dream Recall, Sleep On It! The Practical Side of Dreaming. Sun, Man, Moon, Inc., 1991.

Campbell, Joseph, ed. The Portable Jung. New York City: Penguin Books USA Inc, 1971

Carroll, Lewis. Alice in Wonderland and Through the Looking-Glass. New York: Modern Library, original publication, 1856.

Cayce, Hugh Lynn. Venture Inward: A Guide to the Doorways to Inner Exploration. New York: Harper & Row, 1964.

Corriere, Richard, and Joseph Hart. The Dream Makers: Discovering Your Breakthrough Dreams. New York: Funk & Wagnalls, 1977.

Freud, Sigmund. The Interpretation of Dreams. New York: Avon Books, 1965.

Goldhammer, John D. Radical Dreaming: Use Your Dreams to Change Your Life. New York: Kensington Publishing Corp., 2003.

Garfield, Patricia. Creative Dreaming. New York: Ballantine Psychology, 1975.

Hobson, J. Allan. The Dreaming Brain. New York: Basic Books, 1988.

———. Dreaming: An Introduction to the Science of Sleep. Oxford: Oxford University Press, 2002.

———. Dreaming: A Very Short Introduction. Oxford: Oxford University Press, 2002.

Jung, C. G. Analytical Psychology: Its Theory and Practice. New York: Random House, 1968.

———. Memories, Dreams, Reflections. New York: Vintage Books Edition, originally published in 1963.

Melnick, Jill. The Art of Dreaming: Tools for Creative Dreamwork. San Francisco: Conari Press, 2001.

Mindell, Arnold. Coma: The Dreambody near Death. Portland, Oregon, Tao Tse Press, 2010.

Skutch, Robert. Journey without Distance: The Story behind "A Course in Miracles." Mill Valley, CA: Foundation for Inner Peace, 2001.

Staker, Susan. Waiting for World's End: The Diaries of Wilford Woodruff. Salt Lake City: Signature Books, 1993.

Schucman, Helen. A Course in Miracles. 2nd ed. Mill Valley, CA: Foundation for Inner Peace, 1992.

Stafford, David. Spies beneath Berlin. Woodstock and New York: The Overlook Press, 2002.

Taylor, Jeremy. The Wisdom of Your Dreams. New York: Penguin Group (USA) Inc., 2009.

Tolstoy, Leo. War and Peace. Translated by Richard Pevear and Larissa Volokhonsky. New York: Random House, 2007.

Walden, Kelly Sullivan. It's All in Your Dreams: Five Portals to an Awakened Life. San Francisco: Conari Press, 2013.

Wilber, Ken. A Brief History of Everything. Boston Shambhala Publications Inc., 1996.

Vogel, Steve. Betrayal in Berlin, George Blake, the Berlin Tunnel and the Greatest Conspiracy of the Cold War. London: John Murray (Publishers), 2019.

List of Dreams by Dreamer

List of Spreadsheets

Index

Page numbers followed by (s) refer to spreadsheets.
*Page numbers in **boldface** are definitions.*

About the Authors

Eugene N. Kovalenko is a PhD in engineering science and has had a lifelong interest in intuitive mysticism and psychology. Eugene's training in science and engineering led him to a method of dream analysis that uses a variety of scoring parameters. In 1966, he underwent Jungian analysis, which gave him an enduring appreciation for the significance of dreams. In 1976, he taught an experimental course in dreamwork at UCLA called Creative Dreaming and Spiritual Awakening. He has conducted many CREEI workshops in business, engineering, and community settings, applying THE CREEI PROCESS to personnel and company morale problems. More recently, at the suggestion of a social worker for the Veterans Administration in New Mexico, he began THE CREEI PROCESS pilot program for members of Veterans of Foreign Wars (VFW) suffering from PTSD nightmares. He is presently retired and living with his wife, Birgitta, in New Mexico.

Robert J. Thomsen, MD was a practicing dermatologist in Los Alamos, New Mexico, for nearly thirty-five years. He has always tried to be open to new things, even if he did not understand them. This openness led to deeper experiences of his out-of-awareness self, including learning from Eugene N. Kovalenko THE CREEI PROCESS. Bob is married to Michelle Thomsen, a space physicist, and they have two adult children. He has recorded over eight hundred dreams in his dream journal. One day he offered to help Eugene write up his life work of developing THE CREEI PROCESS so that it could be more widely disseminated, and the result of the collaboration is this book.

CPSIA information can be obtained
at www.ICGtesting.com
Printed in the USA
LVHW090042130122
708466LV00015B/127